# THE CONSTANT CROSS

# The Constant Cross

RUPERT LANGENSTEIN, C.P.

ST. MARY'S MONASTERY
DUNKIRK, N. Y.

THE BRUCE PUBLISHING COMPANY
MILWAUKEE

IMPRIMI POTEST:
    ERNEST WELCH, C.P.
    *Provincialis*

NIHIL OBSTAT:
    JOHN A. SCHULIEN, S.T.D.
    *Censor librorum*

IMPRIMATUR:
    ✠ ALBERT G. MEYER
    *Archiepiscopus Milwauchiensis*

Die 4a Decembris, 1953

# *Introduction*

THROUGHOUT THE COURSE OF OUR LIFETIME, there are countless amazing things which come to our attention. In childhood, we are wide-eyed as we hear of the real or imaginary achievements of our favorite heroes. In our school days, we are captivated by the marvels of nature and of science, a scented, colorful flower springing from a drab and dusty seed, the mysteries of sight and of hearing, the fascinating enigma of radio and of television. Those of us who have the gift of faith are privileged to delve further, beyond the natural evidences of God's creation. And here we find facts, and one fact especially, infinitely more amazing and incredible than anything that nature has to offer. When we ponder the simple statement: God became Man and suffered and died for the salvation of the world — we are dealing with something that seems beyond the boundaries of possibility. It is something so unexpected, so unlikely, and yet, it is something which our faith reveals to us as the simple, incontrovertible truth.

Men react in various ways to the truth of Christ's death for us. The saint replies by actions, and leads a life which shows his gratitude and appreciation for all that God has done for him. He sees the logic and the force of St. Peter's words: "Christ suffered for us, leaving you an example that you should follow in his footsteps." And in the life of every Christian saint, there is the definite impress of a realization of the meaning of Christ's sufferings.

What the saint says by his actions, the writer says with words. The writer may be a saint and should be a saint, but his function as a writer is something quite distinct. Yet, he too feels the impact of God's love for the world. And the Christian writer is led, sooner or later, to consider how a person would react, in certain conditions of life, to a realization of Christ's sufferings and death. The Passion of Christ does, of course, affect every condition and contingency of human life, but it is still somewhat of a revelation to see the range of conditions to which Christian writers have applied it, even in works which are far from being classed as particularly spiritual.

The theme adopted by any writer, his characters, their problems and the way in which they meet them, are necessarily a mirror of some phase of his own life or of his thinking. The case of the famous and popular English novelist, James M. Barrie, is not unique. Barrie's love for his mother was one of the strongest influences in his life; his admiration for her was almost unbounded. Deliberately, he made her the central figure in some of his earlier writings, but when it was suggested to him that he was perhaps overdoing this, he tried to eliminate his mother from his stories. To make sure that he had not failed in his determination, as soon as he finished a manuscript, he would read it to his sister to get her verdict. She would solemnly assure him that there was no reference to his mother, but she said this only to humor him. As soon as she could, she hurried upstairs to where Barrie's mother sat waiting. Breathlessly, she blurted out the news which the old mother was so happy to hear: "You are in again." So, too, is it with the Christian writer, and the story of Christ's sufferings.

The writer of fiction does not claim and will not even admit that any actual happening forms the basis of his writings. He merely wants to show what people would do and say in a given set of circumstances. He is not writing books for spiritual reading, and he is certainly anxious that he should not appear to be doing so. But if he understands the significance of our Lord's sufferings, if he has tried to grasp what they should mean to every single human being, the author has no choice. That knowledge must assert itself over and over again. It is, therefore, a tribute to the Christian character of so many writers of fiction that the significance of Christ's sufferings is evident to them when they are searching for the solution to the problems of their heroes and heroines. So often, they find that there is no other answer or explanation which is really adequate. Frequently, therefore, one could say to Christ in His sufferings what was said to Barrie's mother: "You are in again!"

In the following pages, we will consider some of the varied uses that modern writers of fiction have made of the sufferings of Christ. What we offer will not be book reviews, nor on the other hand will they be sales talks promoting the various authors. Rather, we will consider some of the common, inevitable problems of human life, as we all experience them or see them, and find how similar problems have been described in fiction, and how they have been solved. In most instances, the authors have not made the Passion of Christ the primary and obvious theme of the book. Often, their use of it is rather summary and brief. Often, too, one might almost miss its significance in his preoccupation with the incidents of the story itself. But in all of the books we shall consider, there is a worth-while and practical use of the fact of Christ's sufferings. There is something that can guide our conduct or at least direct our outlook.

Merely to know what others have done, does not, of course, compel us to do likewise. This is true of the example given us by Christ and His saints; and it is much more true of the characters of fiction. If people can be clearly familiar with the life and actions of Christ, if they can know the self-sacrificing lives of the countless heroes of Christianity, and still live their own life in any fashion they choose, then certainly imaginary people with imaginary problems will not compel any great mass movement toward perfection. Even if vast changes cannot be wrought, however, there is no reason for despising lesser improvements. Such improvements should be desirable.

There are many people of good will who need merely to be taught, and they will believe; there are many who need only to be guided and led, and they will follow; and many of these neither know the fact of Christ's sufferings nor the force they should have upon their lives. To all of these, we offer what we have found of guidance and of inspiration in the writings of modern-day authors of fiction. We hope too that the pages of fiction will help to reveal the truth that is stranger than fiction — the truth of our Lord's sufferings and death.

# Acknowledgments

THE AUTHOR WISHES TO EXPRESS HIS GRATI-
tude and appreciation to the respective publishers and authors
for permission to quote from the following books bearing
their imprint: *Pilgrim's Inn* (Elizabeth Goudge; copyright
1948, by Elizabeth Goudge; reprinted by permission of
Coward-McCann, Inc.); *The Diary of a Country Priest*
(Georges Bernanos, Macmillan Company, copyright 1948);
*Out of the Whirlwind* (William Thomas Walsh; Robert M.
McBride Company, by permission of Crown Publishers, Inc.);
*The Cross* (Sigrid Undset; Alfred A. Knopf, Inc.); *Robert
Kimberley* (Frank Spearman; Charles Scribner's Sons); *The
Keys of the Kingdom* (A. J. Cronin; Little, Brown and Com-
pany); *Vipers' Tangle* (François Mauriac; Sheed and Ward,
Inc., New York); *The Chief Mourner of Marne* (from *The
Secret of Father Brown*, by G. K. Chesterton; Harper and
Brothers); *Never No More* (Maura Laverty; Longmans,
Green and Company, Inc.); *Door of Unrest* (O. Henry;
Doubleday and Company, Inc.); *Magnificent Obsession*

## ACKNOWLEDGMENTS

(Lloyd Douglas; Houghton Mifflin Company); *Weeping Cross* (Henry L. Stuart; Henry Regnery Company); *Brideshead Revisited* (Evelyn Waugh; Little, Brown and Company); *Shadow On the Earth* (Owen Francis Dudley; Longmans, Green and Company, Inc., 1952); *How Green Was My Valley* (Richard Llewellyn; Macmillan Company, 1940); *Death Comes for the Archbishop* (Willa Cather; Alfred A. Knopf, Inc.); *Mirror for Toby* (Cecily Hallack; Burns, Oates and Washbourne, Ltd.); *Jesse and Maria* (Enrica von Handel-Mazzetti; Henry Holt and Company, Inc.); *Doomsland* (Shane Leslie, by permission of Sir Shane Leslie, Baronet; published by Chatto and Windus, London); *Father Malachy's Miracle* (Bruce Marshall; Doubleday and Company; Curtis Brown, Ltd.); *A Watch In the Night* (Helen C. White; Macmillan Company, 1935); *The Other Wise Man* (Henry Van Dyke; Harper and Brothers).

# Contents

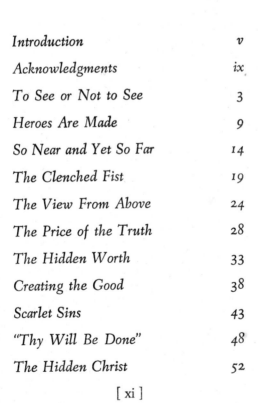

[ xi ]

# CONTENTS

# THE CONSTANT CROSS

# To See or Not to See

THE STORY OF GOD'S LOVE FOR MANKIND, HIS sufferings and death for His human creatures, should be the most familiar fact in the mind of every man, woman, and child. It should be one of the earliest memories of childhood, the restraining influence of youth, the guide in our maturity, and the shining hope of old age. And yet it is anything but that for the vast generality of people. The story of Christ's sufferings not merely fails to impress people as much as it should, but, in many cases, it exerts no influence at all, even among Christians.

Why should this be so? It is not that people remain unimpressed by the love and concern of others. All experience is quite to the contrary. Nor is it that there is an overfamiliarity with our Lord's sufferings, since so many Christians would be unable to identify even the main characters and incidents of the Passion of Christ. It is more likely that many people have simply never given any serious thought to this central fact of Christian belief. Just as they associate with various individuals day after day, work with them, talk with them, without any thought of who they are and where they live and what they live for, so too they may often have come in contact with the fact of our Lord's sufferings without ever thinking of its real meaning for them.

Elizabeth Goudge in *Pilgrim's Inn* portrays a family upon which the fact of Christ's sufferings tried to impress itself. The story describes how this young family purchased an old English inn, and used it as a home. One of the smaller upper rooms had been fitted up with shelves to act as a storeroom. By a combination of circumstances, one of the children of the family who is interested in art discovers that there is a beautiful old fresco under the layers of wallpaper in the storeroom. The room turns out to have been a little chapel in bygone days and the fresco is found to represent the story of St. Placidus.

One of the visitors in the house remembers the story of St. Placidus and tells it to the family. Placidus, the Roman noble, a pagan but a man of good and innocent life, was out hunting one day and saw a white deer which he pursued. Suddenly, so the story goes:

"The deer stopped and swung round to face him, lifting its proud head, and the antlers formed themselves into a gleaming cross, with a crucified Figure upon it, that strange symbol of the Christians which he had seen many times and wondered at for a moment or two, and then had turned aside and gone on his way thinking no more about it. But now he could not turn aside, for the deer, the vision sent to him, had led him directly to this end. His way was blocked by this impassible mountain and the challenge of this cross.

"There was only one thing he could do and he did it. He leaped from his horse and fell upon his knees. And a voice cried out loudly, echoing through the forest, 'Placidus, why doest thou attempt to injure me? I am Jesus Christ whom thou has long served in ignorance. Dost thou believe in me?' And Placidus answered, 'Lord, I believe.' The voice came again, the words spoken this time very low in his own soul, as though in warning, 'Many sorrows shalt thou endure for my sake, many temptations will assail thee, but be of good courage, I will always be with thee.'

"A thrill of dismay went through Placidus, yet he did not hesitate, for he knew that he was not yet at his journey's end; as he had followed the vision of the deer to the vision of the cross, so he must follow the vision of the cross to something beyond again. What it was he still did not know, but in spite of his fear he did know that to attain the goal at last he would give all that he had, down to the last drop of his blood. 'Lord, I am content,' he said. 'Only give me patience to endure all things for Thee.' When at last he looked up again the deer with the crucifix between its antlers had disappeared and night was falling in the forest."

It was a dramatic way for the meaning of the Cross to impress itself upon that group, and it did have some temporary effects. As the author expresses it:

"Their awe deepened the longer they worked, and their happiness too. The thought of this glory, waiting here for so long for rebirth, hidden but safe, was invigorating in these days of anxiety and fear. It was a prophecy, and as such they hugged it to them. Everyone seemed to feel the same. Lucilla and Margaret and Hilary were constantly jolting over in the Ford to see how they were getting on. . . . Malony and Annie-Laurie, though they said little and visited the chapel seldom, looked at it when they did come with a queer sort of frustrated hunger, as though it were offering them something that they did not yet know how to take. . . . George and Nadine put in no work upon the walls, and of all the household were the most detached in their attitude toward the frescoes."

As time passed, however, the whole incident was little more than a memory for any of them. If an event such as this could not radically and permanently alter the life of every individual in a family, it would be hard for anything of a religious nature to have any lasting effects. If even those members of the family who were affected most retained nothing but curiosity or "frustrated hunger" for something they did not "know how to take," then we can well understand why so many people to whom the story of Christ's sufferings is presented with little or no drama are quite unreceptive. How can this be changed? How can people be made to attend and remember? How can they be brought to see the light from which they have so carefully shielded their eyes? There is no simple answer and perhaps no single answer to these questions. It is a riddle which dates back to the day of Calvary, when some could scoff and sneer, some could walk by indifferently, while the Roman centurion, who saw no more than anyone else, could cry out: "Indeed, this was the Son of God."

The difficulty perhaps goes back to childhood. Every child starts out in life with an insatiable curiosity, a ceaseless craving to understand everything. "Why does the sun shine?" "Why does the fire burn?" "Why do I have to sleep?" "Why do I have to eat?" These and a thousand other questions are as natural to every child as it is for him to be a child. But all too soon, this desire to know is sharply

curtailed. Too soon, schoolbooks and classes have become not
a priceless opportunity but rather a necessary burden. Often
the only incentive to learn is the hope of better financial
conditions in the years ahead.

This is the mental outlook which develops so early in
many people and continues on throughout their lifetime.
If they know their job at least well enough to make a living,
if they know how to manage their domestic and financial
affairs well enough to avoid tragedy or discomfort, if they
can enjoy most of the things that their associates are enjoying,
often they ask for no more. If they have received a religious
education which offers them an explanation of life and
their purpose in life, this may fill a greater or lesser part
of their thinking. If, however, that information has been
served to them with little or no effort of their own, there
is often no attempt to seek an answer to the deeper questions
of life: "Who am I? Why am I here? Is there a God, and
if so, is He concerned about my welfare? Is this life all that
we can hope for?" These questions are apparently never
asked or, if they are asked, there is little search for an answer.

In view of this, it is not strange to find that the specific
teachings of religion are so very unfamiliar. There are many
people who still refer to themselves as Christian, and who
feel that they make up a Christian community, who have
only the vaguest notions of Christ — who He is, what He did,
why He did it. They have seen representations of the
crucifix, and they know the cross as a bit of jewelry or as
the pinnacle of a church steeple. They do not know, and
seem not to care, what the real story of the Cross means. It
is not that they are incapable of learning, but they are not
forced to learn, and they do not follow mere opportunities.

This is happening to many people in real life as well as in

fiction. It may be happening to us. But it should not, and it need not. St. John's description of Christ still prevails. "He came unto his own, and his own received him not. But to as many as received him, he gave the power of becoming sons of God."

# Heroes Are Made

IN EVERY GAME OR CONTEST DEVISED BY MAN, there are many who compete or strive against each other, but only one or a few who can win. In fact, the success of one usually demands the defeat of someone else; for every winner there must be a loser. This is true not only of games and sports; it is true of most of the affairs of human life. Often, a man succeeds in business only by taking customers from his fellow businessmen; a man wins a political victory by defeating his opponent; a man gets rich by accumulating the wealth that others had or could have had. There is, in fact, only one contest in which everyone can win. That is the striving to lead a life that is pleasing to God. In this contest every success does not call for a corresponding failure. There *may* be failures and defeat, but there need not be. Moreover, every failure is a tragedy. The really tragic part is the fact that failure is so unnecessary. With a little more effort, a little more striving, a little more use of the help that was available, there would have been success.

There are failures, of course, among Christians of any rank or condition. Even those who know better, do not necessarily act according to their knowledge; and even those who have much more abundant sources of help, do not necessarily use what is available to them. A man can point the way to heaven without going there himself. A learned theologian can fail just as surely and miserably as can an uneducated peasant. Graham Greene, in *The Power and The Glory,* describes the failure which can come even to one who has the greatest of vocations and opportunities. He describes a priest living in the days of darkest persecution in Mexico. When priests were given their choice of renouncing their priesthood and marrying and becoming pensioners of the state or of being savagely put to death as traitors, this man had chosen to remain and carry on his duties. He accepted the status of a man without a country, a man who must travel always in disguise and always in fear of discovery, a man whose duty compelled him to bring spiritual help to his fellow Catholics, but who exposed them as well as himself to great danger by the very fact of approaching them.

It was a life in which the heroic was demanded every day, and in which martyrdom was the inevitable goal. But here, just as much as in any prosaic life, a man was still free. He could be great; he could be mediocre; he could fail. This priest who was called upon to portray the heroic, felt only the cloying weight of his own limitations and failures. His good determinations lacked the vigor which would have brought him to victory. The example of Christ — Christ suffering, Christ dying — is the inspiration of all Christian heroism, but this had been almost forgotten. The price which Christ paid in atoning for sin, His sufferings which keep us from committing sin, His torments which inspire sorrow for the sins which have been committed — all this was far in the background of his thoughts. He kept going on, after a fashion, but the life and inspiration was gone from him. He carried on, day after day, because he felt he must.

The author pictures the climax of this almost heroic life. That priest allowed himself to be betrayed into the hands of his enemies, allowed himself to be seized in the act of ministering to a dying criminal who had called for him. Without the formality of a trial, he was sentenced to death. The moment of execution came closer and closer. His jailer made one slight gesture of human sympathy. Just as the executioners of Christ offered Him vinegar and gall in His dying moments, so he offered his prisoner a little brandy to calm his distress. It was the one act of sympathy or friendship offered to the condemned man. The author describes the approach of the end.

"When he woke up it was dawn. He woke with a huge feeling of hope which suddenly and completely left him at the first sight of the prison yard. It was the morning of his death. He crouched on the floor with the empty brandy flask in his hand trying to remember an act of contrition. 'O God, I am sorry and beg pardon for all my sins . . . crucified . . . worthy of Thy dreadful punishments.' He was confused, his mind was on other things; it was not the good death for which one always prayed. He caught sight of his own shadow on the cell wall: it had a look of surprise and grotesque unimportance. What a fool he had been to think that he was strong enough to stay when others fled. What an impossible fellow I am, he thought, and how useless. I have done nothing for anybody. I might just as well have never lived. His parents were dead — soon he wouldn't even be a memory — perhaps after all he wasn't really Hell-worthy. Tears poured down his face: he was not at the moment afraid of damnation — even the fear of pain was in the background. He felt only an immense disappointment because he had to go to God empty-handed, with nothing done at all. It seemed to him at that moment that it would have been quite easy to have been a saint. It would only have needed a little self-restraint and a little courage. He felt like someone who has missed happiness by seconds at an appointed place. He knew now at the end that there was only one thing that counted — to be a saint."

Perhaps under other circumstances, this man's death could have been different, even if his life had been the same. If he had more time to prepare, if he had someone to speak to him, to encourage him, someone to bring the strength of God's sacraments, things could have ended differently in spite of the neglect that had gone before. But while God does sometimes grant these helps, He does not promise them, even to those who spend their life bringing God's grace to their fellow men. Things could have been different, but they were not. Only God can know the true condition of human hearts; only He can tell who is truly deserving of His love or His hatred. He often allows us, however, to see where those called to the heroic have fallen short.

There is an old saying that "heroes are born not made." This is not really true. Greatness, especially in the more important affairs of human life, is not thrust upon us. God gives us much, but we must work with Him. We must learn to do what is right, willingly and generously, because of God's love for us. We must avoid what is evil because of what Christ's death has revealed about the evil of human sin. We must be sorry for our mistakes and sins because of what Christ suffered for sin. If we do this throughout our lifetime, there will be no fear or uncertainty at life's closing. We cannot fail if we have realized always that "there was only one thing that counted — to be a saint." We cannot fail to be heroic, if our lives have been inspired by the heroism of the suffering Christ.

# So Near and Yet So Far

ONE OF THE MOST REMARKABLE GIFTS THAT
God has given to us is our ability to think and to know. Compared to so many other creatures of God, we are small in size, insignificantly small. Our mind, nevertheless, gives us the power to go far, far beyond this physical limitation. It can reach out and grasp something of the whole, vast universe. Nothing is too great for us, just as nothing is too small. The mind can compare one thing with another; it can discover many of the laws by which the world is governed; it can even predict something of the future.

This amazing power of the human mind should be a source not only of gratification but of gratitude. It is a power that we have not acquired by ourselves; it has been freely given to us. Nor have we created the world of knowledge; we have found it ready-made. Again, we did not originate the laws by which the universe is governed; we have only been able to discover some few of them. In short, even at our best, we are merely getting in contact with something which God has provided for us. Kepler, the world-famous astronomer, expressed it so well when he said: "O God, these are Thy thoughts which I am thinking after Thee."

This is the reaction of the truly learned man, the man who knows his own limitations, the man who realizes that despite the almost limitless power of the human mind, he can contribute but little to this universe. There are those, however, who have a quite different attitude. They do not consider how little they know of what can be known. They do not consider how little of their wisdom is due to themselves. They merely find that there are others with less opportunity for learning or less mental aptitude than they have, and at once they are filled with a sense of their own importance. They know something that some of their fellow men do not know. Therefore, they are as little gods. They are like the country schoolmaster described by Goldsmith in his *Deserted Village,* who seemed such a prodigy among his rustic pupils: "And still they gazed, and still the wonder grew that one small head could carry all he knew."

This foolish and pompous conceit would be laughable were it not for the fact that it is able to cause so much harm. For example, there are at times college professors of this type who are able to dazzle the ignorance of certain of their students, and to extend this foolish self-worship. They can persuade immature minds that they are the source of wisdom and knowledge, and those who disagree are stupid. They are the last authority, and all other authority is a blow at their freedom. They are the ones who must be believed, but belief in God or country or parents is folly. They would not perhaps express it precisely in that way, but it is really the summary of their teaching.

In *The Diary of a Country Priest* by Georges Bernanos, there is described, somewhat in passing, the fruits of this type of teaching. A young man, with some background and training in the Catholic faith, attends a school of medicine. As any intelligent person should know, there is nothing among all the facts of medical discovery that militates against Christianity in any way. On the contrary, it is difficult to see how one could know much about the marvelous functioning of the human body and not be forced to a consciousness of God. Faith will always change a great doctor into a greater doctor. However, this particular young man, Maxence Delbende, like many others, came under the influence of glib, atheistic teachers who were insistent that there could be no God, and who were very willing that they should take God's place. The young doctor left medical school with a good skill in medicine, but no religious faith. He had been given training in the preservation of human life, but had lost the meaning and purpose of his own life. He was a kind man, a man who exerted himself unselfishly for others, but there was nothing left to make it all worth while.

Dr. Delbende's faith was dead, or as good as dead, but he could not remove it entirely from his life. He could not help realizing what he had lost. The author describes him thus:

"But he was inconsolable at not being able to believe. He had some extraordinary ways. He would hurl questions at a crucifix hanging on his bedroom wall. Sometimes he would sob at its feet with his head in his hands, or he would even defy it, shaking his fist."

There is portrayed briefly, but oh, so well, the whole heart of the problem. God does not die when our faith dies. He can be removed from our lives, but He cannot be destroyed. Even the man who has come to hate Him or despise Him knows that his hatred and scorn are not directed at the empty air. They are directed against a personal God.

Moreover, such a man instinctively realizes that somehow or other the Cross of Christ is the point at issue. It is the ultimate condemnation of pride and self-conceit. Christ, the Son of God, who is the very Wisdom of God, humbled Himself, becoming obedient unto death. He, who is to judge heaven and earth, allowed Himself to be condemned by the unjust Pilate. He, who directs the whole universe, allowed soldiers to lead Him whither they would, and even do to Him whatever their savagery suggested. There is no excuse for men to set themselves up as gods, when God allows Himself to become the slave of man.

That truth may be accepted or rejected, but it still exists. It exists for our instruction and guidance. God has given us the gift of intelligence and we must ever strive to make good use of it. But there comes a point where our natural intelligence cannot guide us, and we must proceed by faith, if we are to proceed at all. There are depths of knowledge whither our minds cannot penetrate, and we must be guided by the superior knowledge of God. That is the hurdle which is the downfall of so many. If they will not submit to the infinite wisdom of God, they are exposed to limitless error. The story of Christ's sufferings, however, removes all shame and repugnance from such submission. If God could submit to our human judgments, we should not hesitate to submit to Him.

The loss of faith is an extreme thing, a terrible thing, and fortunately a rather unusual thing. Yet it does happen, not only to the uninstructed but often to those who have had great opportunities for learning. All of us should be determined to safeguard and increase our own faith, but that should not content us. We should be zealous also to counter-act the evil of those who are driving the spirit of faith from the hearts of our fellow men. There are men who still hurl questions at the crucifix, still defy it, still shake their fist at it with senseless and impotent rage. We should help them to see the futility of all this, help them to kneel before the crucifix, to worship, and to submit and to believe.

# The Clenched Fist

IN A RECENT POPULAR PLAY, A NUMBER OF the characters are inmates of an institution for the mildly insane. One of these is a woman with a hate obsession. On the slightest provocation, she will launch into a list of her hates: "I hate everything in the world, but most of all I hate cold cream, hot dogs, codfish, crawfish, catfish, catnip, sheep-dip, sawdust . . ." and so on and on. Such a recital from such a person in such a setting arouses in us an amusement mixed with pity. Like all the rantings of the insane, it is not taken seriously. It is an unfortunate affliction. However, all of us come in contact, from time to time, with hatred that is just as intense, just as bitter, just as unreasoning, hatred which cannot be overlooked or brushed lightly aside. It is the hatred begotten of prejudice and ignorance and bigotry. It is a hatred which seems never to die, and will not be content unless it can destroy everything else.

People obsessed with this spirit of hatred are seldom content to keep it to themselves. The infection must be spread. They labor unceasingly to create in others a hatred of God and the creatures of God, a hatred of all the purposes of God. They seem determined to produce bitterness and ill feeling everywhere and at any cost.

Sometimes, their approach is quite evident; at other times, it is rather subtle. In times of war, they can come into the open with slogans of hatred along nationalistic lines, and no one will dare to oppose them: "Hate the Japs! Hate the Germans! Hate the Russians!" At other times, they will call for religious hatred: "Hate Catholics! Hate Protestants! Hate Jews!" depending upon the faction which is expected to do the hating.

Usually, however, the approach must be a little more gradual. The hatred must be coated over, at least at first. It must be made to seem reasonable. A spirit of loyalty, or a spirit of self-protection or self-interest, must be introduced to make the hatred seem inevitable. That is the procedure, repeated over and over, which is always able to add new fuel to the fire, and keep the pot of hatred boiling vehemently. The agents of hatred are not many, but there are always enough of them to carry on the deadly work. They work so effectively that those who are whipped up to a frenzy of hatred scarcely ever realize that they are the victims of vicious distortion of truth.

This method was used successfully by the enemies of Christ nineteen hundred years ago. Our Lord was popular with the people. He had done nothing but good for them. No one could come out and urge the public to hate Christ. It simply would not have worked. With the indirect approach, however, it was quite easy. The word was spread that Christ would not be of help to the interests of the nation. He might favor the oppressing Romans, even though He had clearly insisted that His followers must render to Caesar only what was Caesar's, and to God what was God's. Or, on the other hand, He might provoke the Romans into taking away what little remained of Jewish freedom.

The reasons given to the multitude were not very clear. They didn't have to be. Most slanderous reports are not very clear anyway. Christ was a danger, and it was their duty to stand together. Justly or unjustly, He must be put to death. The mob that cried out: "Crucify Him" on the first Good Friday were not automatons or puppets; but they were certainly not expressing their own feelings. They had been carefully worked up to this pitch of hatred.

It is perhaps useless to speculate about what might have been. It is futile to consider what a difference it would have made for the Jewish nation, the Chosen People of God, if they had seen through this deception; if they had questioned those who were trying to stir them to hatred and investigated their motives; if they had realized that their primary loyalty was not to a pack of unscrupulous politicians, but to God and to their own conscience. If that had happened, the Jewish nation would have fulfilled the destiny and purpose which God had assigned to it. Its religious life would have come to full flowering and development. Down through the succeeding centuries, the good Jew would never have been pitted against the good Christian, or vice versa.

William Thomas Walsh, in his novel *Out of the Whirlwind*, puts a realization of all this into the mind of one of his characters. A Jew, Henry Kaplan, has taken an interest in a Catholic young man who is in prison. He agrees to obtain a crucifix for him, and does so at some embarrassment and inconvenience to himself. Alone in his office, Kaplan looks at the crucifix closely, and its significance forces itself into his consciousness. He speaks to the Man on the Cross.

"You were a Jew like us, and You suffered more than any of us. You suffered as much as anybody could suffer. It was a cruel thing, that's what it was. A cruel thing. We did, we Jews did. It's all baloney about the Romans doing it. If I tell somebody to kill a man, I can't say it's all *his* fault. What did we do it for? You were a Jew, like us, and a noble Jew. It was just what I was saying this afternoon about Greenhut — the high priests did a dirty day's work, and we covered them up, and let the blame be put on us, just because they were Jews, instead of kicking them out and following our own conscience. And we shouldn't always blame You for what the Christians do to us. That's their fault, not Yours. You never told them to do it. You told them just the opposite. Christians! Some of us Jews are better Christians than they are."

If all Christians and Jews could see the basis of the problem as clearly as this, there would be few problems to solve. There is evil in the world, there are evil men, and all evil must be hated. But that is not what motivates the professional promoters of hatred. With them, hatred is a tool, a weapon which they use for their own sinister purposes, and they find it is not too difficult to do this. Well do we speak of hatred as *blind* hatred; for it can keep a person from seeing even the most obvious truth.

It is important that we realize that anyone can be misled. No one is automatically immune to hatred or bigotry or prejudice; but if we recognize the evil, and know that it is evil, there is a minimum of danger to ourselves.

It is not probable that the spirit of hatred will ever be eliminated from human living. It is an evil plant which not only finds fertile soil but willing hands to tend it. It is well to remember nonetheless that we are never really the victims of this spirit of hatred unless we allow it to infect us. Just as hatred opposed Christ, tortured Him, killed Him, but never overcame Him, so too, we do not become its victims, no matter what it does to us, unless we admit it into our hearts and lives.

# The View From Above

IT HAS OFTEN BEEN SAID THAT TO LIVE IN THE Church established by Christ is difficult, but to die in it is wonderful. This, like so many sayings, would not find everyone in complete agreement. There are many who do not find a Christian life particularly difficult. In fact, those who try faithfully to do what God wants are agreed: "My yoke is sweet and my burden is light." We can all observe that those who have the most to say about the difficulty in God's laws are those who have never really tried to live up to them.

Nevertheless, in itself the Christian life is not an easy thing. It requires sacrifice and self-restraint and patience; but these, though unattractive to most of us, are certainly not beyond our possibilities if we use the help that God puts at our disposal. If we had merely a pagan outlook on life, and acted entirely from natural and selfish motives, then we would be attempting the impossible; but with a Christian view of life, and with the help of Christ and His Church, it is quite different. If we are deeply conscious of the fact that we have God's understanding and His help, we approach the Christian life with confidence of success. There will, of course, always be problems we cannot solve and questions we cannot answer, but that does not make life a hopeless riddle. God knows all things. He knows them individually with all their particular circumstances. He knows the minor and incidental details of all life better than we know the things we have made the object of specialized study. More important still, God sees every person and every happening in its relation to everything else. That is perhaps why He permits temporary evils and frustrations to come to His friends. He can see a present evil disposing people and things for a future good; furthermore, He is able to provide, in His own way and in His own time, for whatever necessities the future may bring.

In *The Cross,* Sigrid Undset has one of her major characters, Kristin Lavransdatter, realizing this clearly toward the end of her life. Kristin had lived a long and eventful Catholic life. She had known the successes and disappointments which any life can bring, the moments of joy and the hours of sorrow. There had been many plans for herself and her husband, many hopes for her children, and, as in all planning and hoping, there had been a mingling of accomplishment and disappointment. She had usually meant well, but she had made mistakes, serious mistakes at times. There had, on occasion, been lack of purpose and lack of direction. In her last days, with her husband dead and her children gone out of her life, she was glad when she had the opportunity to enter a convent to prepare for life's ending.

Then it was that she saw her life in its true perspective. "It seemed to her," as the author tells us, "that she had come to look out over her life in a new way: as when a man comes upon a height above his native place where he has never climbed before, and looked down from it into his own dale. He knows each farm and fence, each thicket, the gully of each beck; but he seems to see for the first time how these things all lie on the face of the land. And seeing things in this new way, she had found all at once words that swept away both her bitterness against Erlend (her husband) and her terrors for his soul, borne off by sudden death. Ill-will he had never borne to any; she saw it now, and God had seen it always.

"So at last she was come so far that she deemed she could look on her own life as from the uppermost steep of a glen. Now did her road lead down into the darkling valley, but ere she took that road she had been given grace to understand that, in the loneliness of the cloister and at the gates of death, there waited for her one who had ever beheld the life of mankind as men's parishes look, seen from the mountain brow. He had seen the sin and sorrow, the love and hate, in the hearts of men, as one sees the rich manors and the humble cots, the teeming cornfields and the abandoned wastes, all borne on the bosom of the same countryside. And He had descended, His feet had trodden the peopled lands, and stood in palaces and in huts; He had gathered up the sorrows and the sins of rich and poor, and lifted them aloft with Him upon a cross."

That is the picture of God and His attitude toward us which should be the great strengthening force of every life. God sees. God understands. God is still in control of His world and of all His creatures. God sees the particular actions of His people, but He sees them as part of a complete picture. He Himself is part of that picture. He has come into our midst. He has "gathered up the sorrows and the sins of rich and poor, and lifted them aloft with Him upon a cross."

Nothing is beyond His understanding or His help. He sees everything and everyone in perfect proportion. That is an understanding of God that never comes to many; an understanding that comes only at the twilight of life to so many others; an understanding that we should have had from the beginning and throughout our life. It is an understanding that is offered to every Christian child, but so often there is no comprehension or acceptance. It is late, or even too late, when he learns to really grasp its meaning, and apply it to his life.

There are many people who feel that heaven alone is God's sphere of interest and influence; the world is ours. "God's in His heaven, all's right with the world" is their attitude. But that is not God's attitude or procedure. He has commanded us to live our lives in a certain way, He has given us definite laws, He has specified our duties to Him and to each other. Having done this, He could have simply rewarded those who obeyed, and punished those who offended. Instead, He became Man and entered our world and our life to help us bring order out of disorder, and peace out of strife. He does not will the conflict and chaos that He finds, but neither is He dismayed by it. He knows that whether it be individuals or families or nations that go astray, there is always a way to restore all things.

Down through the years, many religious writers have seen a special significance in Christ being raised upon His cross. They have seen the Cross offering to Christ an elevated position from which He can view His world in greater detail. But beyond what the Cross offered to Christ, there is something that it should bring to us — the unfailing reminder that God does see, does understand our problems, and has suffered and died to relieve them.

# The Price of the Truth

THERE ARE FEW THINGS IN THIS WORLD AS cheap and as plentiful as human opinions. "Here is what I think," or "Why don't you do it like this," or some similar phrase, would certainly rank among the most frequently used expressions in any language. People have their own ideas about almost everything that has been done or could be done. Sometimes there are nearly as many different opinions as there are people who express them.

Because of this, there are many people who feel that there is little, if anything, that is really certain. They feel that even if one person's opinion is not as good as another's, it would be hard to determine who is right and who is wrong. They do not confine this moreover to things where some uncertainty is inevitable. They are not perfectly sure of anything. In the things of God, just as much as in the things of men, they feel that no one can be perfectly and unhesitantly certain. To them, it is all a matter of opinion, a matter of what they want to believe or find it convenient to accept.

True Christianity has always set itself squarely against that attitude. There are things that are true and things that are false; there are things that are good and things that are bad. In all the important things, we can know which is which. Pilate could say to Christ: "What is truth?" and think that he was dismissing the whole question as an insoluble enigma. Christ, however, knew what truth was and He was willing to die for the truths which He had come into this world to teach. In fact, that was exactly what did bring Him to His death. If He had not condemned the evils of His day, if He had not insisted that His followers practice the unpopular virtues of poverty and humility, if He had not declared that He was truly the Son of God, He would not have carried the cross to Golgotha. He could have enjoyed unending popularity, unending to the extent that any popularity is unending. But He knew that the popularity which He might have enjoyed was not worth the price that must be paid. It was better to lead twelve men with infallible certitude than to receive the shallow plaudits of twelve thousand. It was better to die for what was true than to live for what was false.

Christ's attitude must ever be the attitude of all His true followers. That is why the Church has always had its martyrs. Our Lord paid a price of infinite worth to transmit the truth to His followers, but His followers have added their share to that price. They have "filled up what was wanting to the sufferings of Christ." They have died rather than yield their beliefs to the opinions or prejudices of the day. Men may fight for their opinions. They seldom die for them. In contrast, almost every truth of faith and morals has been defended unto death.

In the novel *Robert Kimberly*, by Frank Spearman, this

unending struggle has been well pictured. Lambert, one of the characters, is a man who considers himself a Catholic, but not what he calls a "clerical." By that, he means that he accepts only those truths which he feels it is modern and fashionable to accept. His attitude is challenged by another man, Kimberly, who is not a Catholic, but does know the history of the Church:

"You a Catholic?" Kimberly echoed slowly. "Oh, no; this is a mistake. . . . You say you were born a Catholic. And you ridicule the very corner-stone of your faith. The last time I met you, you were talking the same sort of stuff. I wonder if you have any idea what it has cost humanity to give you the faith you sneer at, Lambert? To give you Catholic parents, men nineteen hundred years ago allowed themselves to be nailed to crosses and torn by dogs. Boys hardly seven years old withstood starvation and scourging and boys of fifteen were burned in pagan amphitheatres that you might be born a Christian; female slaves were thrown into boiling oil to give you the privilege of faith; delicate women died in shameful agonies and Roman maidens suffered their bodies to be torn to pieces with red-hot irons to give you a Christian mother — and you sit here tonight and ridicule the Resurrection of Christ. Call yourself liberal, Lambert; call yourself enlightened; call yourself Modern, but for God's sake don't call yourself a Catholic."

It would not be easy to say how many men and women of this age, or of any age, deserve the same indictment that this man received. The evil is there, but it is not evident how deep or how extensively it has spread its roots. On occasion, however, perhaps most of us do encounter this attitude. We meet business or professional men who are shamefaced and apologetic about the practice of their religion; we meet col-

lege students who publicly apologize to shallow-minded professors for their Church which is old fashioned enough to
insist upon the laws of God; we meet half-educated social
leaders who retain the name of Catholic, but have allowed
their faith to wither and die. We meet those who are so far
from suffering and dying for their faith, that even the
slightest effort on behalf of their faith is too much for them.

This is a discouraging and disappointing picture of the
Church, but fortunately it is only one small part of a bigger
and better picture. The spirit of faith has never died out,
and today it is perhaps stronger than it has been for centuries.
For example, letters from missionary priests and Sisters and
Brothers show that calm certainty of faith that is so beautiful
a replica of Christ's own assurance. These men and women
are human enough to prefer life to death, to prefer freedom
to imprisonment and torture; but they are superhuman and
Christian enough to accept these latter possibilities if this is
the price they must pay. They know what God has revealed,
and like Christ they will die before they will yield.

Even in the less spectacular and less heroic spheres of
activity the same spirit asserts itself. It is easy to live a shallow,
materialistic, pagan sort of life. It is easy to live marriage on
that level. It is easy to fall into that sort of family spirit. It is
easy, but it is not necessary or inevitable. Far more than most
people realize, there are those who are struggling against the
current, those who are keeping the spirit of Christ alive and
vibrant in modern life.

That is the spirit that is expected and required of each of
us. It is the attitude we must have if we are to keep from
compromising our beliefs and our lives. The heroism of Christ
in accepting the terrible death of the cross, in preference to
yielding the truths He was teaching, could seem above and

beyond our capabilities. It could seem that way, unless we had been shown so clearly that others have done, others are doing, all that is required of us.

# The Hidden Worth

WHENEVER WE SEE ANYTHING, THERE IS A wave of light that comes to our eye and tells a story of something that exists outside. There are shorter waves and longer waves. They tell us where things are and what they look like. They give us a clear report of all the different colors and tints that are the ingredients of beauty. Likewise is it with regard to sound. There are limitless variations in the pitch of sounds. Each variation is reported by waves of different length. Each sound wave comes to the ear, prepared to submit its account of some activity that exists outside. But every eye and ear is limited. For all of us, there is light that we cannot see, and sound that we cannot hear. A report is brought to us, but we do not perceive it. For all practical purposes, it is as if the light were shining in darkness, "and the darkness does not comprehend it." If we should surmount these limitations we must not rely upon ourselves alone, we must make use of the devices which make it possible to perceive the otherwise unseeable light and to hear the otherwise inaudible sounds.

It is somewhat the same with our observation of our fellow men, and even with our knowledge of ourselves. There are some facts about others that we can all perceive at a glance; there are other more important facts which we could never discover if left to ourselves. No one can specify all the various channels by which this knowledge comes to us or tries to come to us. How many of us ever arrive at a perfect knowledge of ourselves, to say nothing of a perfect knowledge of others? Many people live and die, complete strangers not only to others but to themselves. Perception is possible, but most people do not know how to see the true nature and worth of themselves or of others. That is, perhaps, why so few people are inclined to exert themselves much on behalf of others. They do not see anything there that is worth the effort. Even when one has glimpsed the worth that is present in every human being, there are many factors and many people trying to persuade us that what we have seen is imaginary. They would persuade us that it is foolish idealism that is better discarded and forgotten.

In any of the professions in life that call for renouncement of one's own preferences and dedication to the welfare of others, one cannot fulfill his duties unless he keeps before him the sight of what is worth while in his fellow men. We cannot spend our life and our talents for others unless we are convinced that they are worth the sacrifice. In *The Keys of the Kingdom,* A. J. Cronin describes a young priest in the first days of his ministry. Fr. Francis Chisholm was sent to a parish where the response to his efforts was particularly discouraging. Three times a week he had to bicycle to two distant wretched hamlets, to say Mass, hear confessions, and take the catechism class in the local town hall. The lack of response among his people increased his difficulties. The very children were lethargic, shuffling. There was much poverty, heart-rending destitution; the whole parish seemed steeped in apathy, savorless and stale. Passionately he told himself he would not surrender to routine. Conscious of his clumsiness and inefficiency, he had a burning desire to reach these poor hearts, to succor and revive them. He would kindle a spark, blaze the dead ashes into life, if it were the last thing he did.

What made it worse was the fact that the parish priest, astute and watchful, seemed to sense, with a kind of grim humor, the difficulties his curate was experiencing, and to anticipate slyly a readjustment of the other's idealism to his own practical common sense. Once when Francis came in, tired and wet, having bicycled ten miles through wind and rain to an outlying sick call at Broughton, Father Kezer compressed his attitude into a single gibe. " 'Handing out halos isn't what you thought it was — eh?' He added, naturally: 'A good-for-nothing lot.'

"Francis flushed hotly, 'Christ died for a good-for-nothing lot.'

"Deeply upset, Francis began to mortify himself. At meals he ate sparingly, often only a cup of tea and some toast. Frequently, when he woke up in the middle of the night, tortured by misgivings, he would steal down to the church. Shadowed and silent, washed in pale moonlight, the bare edifice lost its distracting crudity. He flung himself down on his knees, begging for courage to embrace the tribulations of this beginning, praying with impetuous violence. At last, as he gazed at the wounded figure on the cross, patient, gentle, suffering, peace would fill his soul."

The remembrance of Christ's sufferings and death is the most powerful aid toward a realization of the value of our fellow man. God is not mistaken in His estimate of anyone or of anything, and when God chose to suffer and die for the salvation of every human creature, He provided the best proof of how great is their worth. At times, in our dealings with others, we glimpse something of this for ourselves, and we may feel that we need no other assurance. But, inevitably, the words or the example of others will take its toll; or perhaps the failure of our plans for others, their lack of co-operation or appreciation will chill our enthusiasm. We may feel that those who are cynical and calloused in their attitude toward others, really have the right outlook. At times such as this, there is nothing so reassuring as the remembrance of God's opinion of our fellow man. If He died for others, we can work for them.

It is not strange or unusual that our perception of others should need some special support. We are limited in all of our perceptions, but here, as in other things, we should not be content with our limitations. Just as we devise glasses to improve and perfect our ordinary seeing; just as we invent microscopes that we may see the tiny world that is normally invisible to us; just as we develop telescopes that carry our vision far beyond the range of normal sight; just as we try to overcome the limitation of hearing — so too should we try to develop and perfect our knowledge of others. Actually, far less ingenuity is required to bring this ability to perfection, to discover what makes others worthy of God's love and ours, to see what makes us deserving of love. God has provided the means ready-made. A knowledge of Christ Suffering offers that ability to see. It shows us Christ not only dying for His friends but pleading with His Father for the forgiveness of His enemies. "Father, forgive them, for they know not what they do." It shows us Christ making a saint out of a criminal who seemed to have only one small requirement for holiness — that he wanted to be a saint. Jesus said to him: "This day thou shalt be with me in Paradise."

An insight into the possible goodness of every human creature is not self-deception. Neither does it unfit us for the demands of everyday life. Rather, it removes from us that spirit of cynicism, that attitude of frustration, that sense of hatred that poisons so much of human relationships. It gives basis for the fulfillment of Christ's command that we must love one another. If Christ could perceive in any one of us enough goodness to make it worth while for Him to suffer and die, then we can learn to perceive enough goodness in others to make it worth while bearing with them, helping them, doing good to them. We need not hide the truth of others' shortcomings: we need only realize the more important truth of their value, a value which is always evident to God, and can be evident to us.

# Creating the Good

IT IS ONE OF THE BIG DISILLUSIONMENTS OF life to find that very often people are not what they seem to be. Even heroes are not always heroic; and the average man or woman is much less so. Often, we may idealize someone as big and brave and completely successful, only to find that he is not even able to face the difficulties of everyday existence. Often, we may find that the man who seems to represent all that is noble and honest has more than his share of human weakness and sin. The outward appearance does not always conform to what is really there. Sometimes it is as if the truth were obscured or even completely masked out.

The reason for this condition is quite simple. There are many people who will never allow themselves to appear as they really are. They know their faults. They know they should be better and could be better, but instead of really improving their lives, they are content to appear better than they are.

In the book, *Vipers' Tangle*, François Mauriac creates a character, a boy named Louis, who resents this tendency to conceal human faults and limitations. This young man has the faculty of seeing himself and others as they really are. He refuses either to gloss over his faults or do anything about them. From childhood right on to old age, he allows others to see him in his true colors. He is mean in money matters, and he allows his family to see it, despising their contempt. He is harsh and domineering, and does not care who sees or knows. He feels little love or affection for anyone, and does not make the effort to pretend otherwise. As might be expected, his life is filled with bitterness, hatred, and frustration. He is not a hypocrite. He feels he is being honest. But he is far from happy. He becomes an outcast in the midst of his own family, suspecting and suspected, hating and being hated. He craves, as does every human creature, for affection and love and understanding, but he cannot believe that anyone is able to give him these things. He will not pretend to be better than he appears to himself. He cannot see anything in himself that would allow others to love him. It does not even occur to him that he could change, could improve, could make himself deserving of the love of God and man.

Such an outlook on life is so foolish even though it seems to be honest and realistic. It sees what is, but it does not see what can be. It is like a man looking at a house that has fallen into disrepair. If he sees only its present condition, he may turn from it in dismay; but if he can picture its possibilities, what he can do to restore and improve it, he may put himself into debt and undergo almost endless toil to bring his dream to reality.

There is really no point at which it becomes completely impossible for a human being to turn from evil to good, to change from what he is to what he can become. If the transformation is too long delayed, it might seem impossible, so that one will not make the necessary effort. It was thus with Louis as described by Mauriac. As an old man, he soliloquized thus:

"What madness, at sixty-eight, to hope to swim against the stream, to impose upon them a new idea of the man that, nevertheless, I am, that I always have been! We only see what we are accustomed to seeing. You, too, my poor children, I do not see you either.

"If I were younger, the lines would be less marked, the habits less deeply rooted; but I doubt whether, even in my youth, I could have broken the spell of this enchantment. One needed some strength, I said to myself, What kind of strength? SOMEONE.

"Yes, Someone in Whom we are all one, Who would be the guarantor of my victory over myself, in the eyes of my family; Someone Who would bear witness for me, Who would have relieved me of my foul burden, Who would have assumed it. . . .

"Even the elect do not learn to love all by themselves. To get beyond the absurdities, the failings, and above all the stupidity of people, one must possess a secret of love which the world has forgotten. So long as this secret is not redis-covered, you will change human conditions in vain."

Here was a man, living in the midst of a Christian family and a Christian community. He was a man who had lived most of his life before he even knew his problem and even then he did not seem to realize that it could be solved. He knew that he needed Someone to bear witness for him, to witness that there still lived within him the seeds of goodness. He knew that He needed Someone to relieve him of the burden of his sins, but he seemed hardly to realize that pardon had been offered, and that he needed only to accept it. God had seen the value and importance and worth that is present in every human soul, and He had so loved the world as to send His only-begotten Son to become man and to save the world. Men are not naturally good in themselves. They must become good by accepting grace from God. We are loved by God not only for what we are, but for what He can make of us.

This man, whose life was distorted and warped because he did not know the meaning of Christ's sufferings and death, lived only in the realm of fiction. His tragedy, how-ever, is not fictitious. It is a real, all too prevalent malady. If the evil is not as apparent as it might be, this is because so many people are not as candid as was Louis.

Most men fall short of what they could be and would like to be, but no one of us is obliged to remain as he is. Our faults are not irrevocably welded to us. Nor is the solution to gloss over our shortcomings, but to correct them. That is what Christ has made possible by His sufferings and death. "Though your sins be as scarlet, they shall be made as white as snow." Not only do the sufferings of Christ make it possible for our sins to be taken away, but they provide the strength and the grace to make us better and to avoid the repetition of former faults. Christ does not merely relieve us of the foul burden of our sins, suffering and atoning on our behalf, but He is also the One who guarantees our victory over self. With His help, we can become such that we can allow others to see us as we are, and feel that they can still find us worthy of their affection and love.

The literature of every country abounds in stories about the discovery of hidden treasure. In most of these stories, the pattern is pretty much the same. Some valuable treasure has been hidden or lost, and no one suspects its presence, no one except the lucky individual who is the hero of the story. He uses his knowledge. He seizes his opportunity. He finds the secret to wealth and power. In real life, it is somewhat the same. There is hidden goodness in us and in others that needs to be discovered. More important still is the possible goodness that will never exist unless we bring it into existence. If we apply the story of God's love for us to our own lives, we will love God as He intends that we should; if we do our part for others, God's love will abundantly enter their lives. We are not merely able to discover goodness. We are privileged to be able to work with God in creating it. We will do this if the infinite goodness of God suffering, God dying, is made the inspiration of our life and actions.

# Scarlet Sins

ONE OF THE MOST COMMON WORDS IN OUR language is the word "accident." It is a simple word that expresses a most important fact, the fact that many of the most harmful and destructive of human actions are not really intended at all. They are accidents. They just happen. They are the result of carelessness or thoughtlessness or inexperience. We all realize this. That is why we are usually willing to make allowances for the things that befall us by accident, and for the harm that people do to us unintentionally. We know that some of these things are inevitable. We know too that we ourselves often cause harm or offense without meaning to do so.

What is hard, if not impossible for us to attain, however, is the forgiveness of those who are quite deliberate in the harm they do. If someone purposely chooses to oppose us or to injure us, our instinctive reaction is to say: "If that is the way he wants it, that is the way he will have it." If someone has acted treacherously toward us, it might hardly cross our mind to accept him back with wholehearted forgiveness, despite anything he might say or do. It is this deeper forgiveness, however, that God shows so often toward all of us.

As far as God is concerned, the only time that any violation of His laws is absolutely final is when death comes along before a person repents. Up to that time, there is no sin that cannot be forgiven. That does not detract from the evil of sin or make it any less serious. It does not make it less foolish or reprehensible for a person to offend God. It does not make it less reckless for a person to take a chance on being eternally separated from God if he does not get the chance or the inclination to repent. It does show clearly the extremes of God's mercy when He is willing to accept the repentance of those who have deliberately rejected Him and His laws.

God's mercy toward us is not based upon an ignorance of our faults or a closing of His eyes to them. Rather, He knows and has proved so often in the past what possibilities of greatness there are even in the most ignoble, what possibilities for holiness even in the most offensive and sinful.

G. K. Chesterton was a writer who was always deeply conscious of this fact. Even in the most unlikely places, in the midst of so many of his detective stories, this thought asserted itself again and again. For example, his story, *The Chief Mourner of Marne,* is concerned with a man who had deliberately arranged to duel with a close relative and friend and then treacherously killed him when the other man thought the duel was over. Father Brown, who solved the case, discusses it with some people who were friends both of the dead man and his assassin. Before they have heard the facts, and think that the case simply involved one man killing another in a duel, they are very tolerant, insisting there is little to forgive. But when they have found that treachery and murder are involved, one of them cries out, " 'You don't expect us to be able to pardon it.' He stood up abruptly and looked round at them. 'We have to touch such men, not with a barge pole, but with a benediction,' he said. 'We have to say the word that will save them from hell. We alone are left to deliver them from despair when your human charity deserts them. Go on your own primrose path pardoning all your favourite vices and being generous to your fashionable crimes; and leave us in the darkness, vampires of the night, to console those who really need consolation; who do things really indefensible, things that neither the world nor they themselves can defend; and none but a priest will pardon. Leave us with the men who commit the mean and revolting and real crimes; mean as St. Peter when the cock crew, and yet the dawn came.' 'The dawn,' repeated Mallow doubtfully. 'You mean hope — for *him?*' 'Yes,' replied the other. 'Let me ask you one question. You are great ladies and men of honour and secure of yourselves; you would never, you can tell yourselves, stoop to such squalid treason as that. But tell me this. If any of you had so stooped, which of you, years afterwards, when you were old and rich and safe, would have been driven by conscience or confessor to tell such a story of yourself? You say you could not commit so base a crime. Could you confess so base a crime?' "

In this, as in so many of his stories, Chesterton makes a very important point. Few men are totally good; no one is completely bad. Not everyone has the same evil inclinations, the same temptations, just as not everyone has the same virtues or good qualities. We often are severe with certain faults and sins simply because they are not our shortcomings, while we can be very tolerant of the weaknesses that exist in our own lives and characters. To have this attitude, however, is an evidence of immaturity. We know that to a child, people are usually placed at one extreme or the other. Children cannot usually reconcile the presence of flaws in those who are good, just as they cannot find good in those who appear evil to them. As we grow older and observe things, however, we find that "the just man falls seven times in a day," and we also find that Christ has "come to call, not the just, but sinners to repentance." We learn that it is only when this earthly life has completed its course, that the evil is completely purged from the lives of the good; it is only then that the last seeds of goodness present in the lives of the evil, are finally rendered sterile.

This is, of course, a strictly Christian attitude and approach. It requires us to expect something close to the miraculous, and miracles do not occur in unaided nature. A doctor usually knows how much he can hope for from his efforts and remedies, but the Christian knows that the power of God can bring life from death itself. The moral guide knows about how much can be accomplished by instruction, guidance, good example, and good environment, but the Christian knows that God's grace can intervene decisively even when all of these have done their best. We, therefore, of all people, are firmly convinced that "while there is life, there is hope." The Apostle Peter committed the almost unpardonable sin of denying Christ, repudiating Him. Yet, today, he is "Saint" Peter, the Prince of the Apostles, the Keeper of the Keys of the Kingdom of Heaven. He is the proof that God can forgive the unforgivable, and does forgive. He is the evidence that any forgiveness need never be in vain.

We must realize that St. Peter was not an isolated example. Every saint has experienced in a similar way the depths of God's forgiveness; every sinner must experience it, if he is not to die in his sins. Moreover, it is not only in God's dealings with us, but also in our dealings with one another that the spirit of forgiveness must shine forth. We ask God to forgive us our trespasses as we forgive those who trespass against us, and so we stand or fall by our spirit of wholehearted forgiveness. All Christian living is elevated by learning the spirit of forgiveness that Christ showed in His Sacred Passion. It is amazing but it is in reality only the fulfillment of Christ's prophecy: "And I, if I be lifted up from the earth, will draw all things unto myself."

# *"Thy Will Be Done"*

WHEN PEOPLE OF A RELIGIOUS TURN OF MIND consider the sort of life they are leading, when they consider the good they are trying to do, and consider also their failures and mistakes, they often find that they have neglected to pray as much as they should. It is a fault and they recognize it as such, but certainly it seems to them just about the least of their failings. In one sense this is right. It is not a very serious thing if we forget to say grace before or after meals, or if we happen to forget to say our morning or evening prayers on some particular occasion. But the danger, the very real danger is that sometimes our neglect of prayer may become greater and greater. It is not only in the morning and night that people sometimes forget God and what they owe to God, or not only at mealtimes — but they live their whole day, they live weeks and months in forgetfulness of Him. They allow all thought of God, and all influence of God to depart entirely from their lives. When that happens, then anything can happen. When life is not dedicated to God, it can be dedicated to almost anyone or anything.

We have a striking example of this occurring in the course of our Lord's Sacred Passion. At the Last Supper, Christ changed bread and wine into His body and blood, and gave His Apostles their first Holy Communion. He foretold that one of them would deny Him, and that all of them would abandon Him. The Apostles, however, from Peter down to the last of them, insisted that they would always be loyal to Him. They would, if necessary, go with Him to suffering and to death. That was their state of mind as the Apostles left the Supper Room with Christ. That was their determination as they passed through the dark, narrow streets of the old city, out to the Garden of Olives. They were sure of themselves, certain just how they would act, but Christ knew that their good intentions and their determination were not enough. Therefore, when He reached the Garden of Gethsemani, and put Himself in prayer to prepare Himself to accept the terrible ordeal of suffering that lay before Him, He commanded them also to prepare themselves for what lay before them — to renew their devotion and dedication to whatever God might send. "Watch and pray, that you enter not into temptation," was Christ's command to them. It was the end of a long, hard day, a day of emotional strain and of unexpected happenings. The Apostles were not in the mood for prayer, and they did not pray, despite Christ's command. While Christ prayed, they slept, although He twice aroused them and repeated His exhortation to prayer.

How different the course of Christ's Sacred Passion would have been if the Apostles had heeded our Lord's warning! How different it would have been for Christ, how different for the Apostles themselves. How much it would have meant for Christ to have His Apostles loyally and fearlessly at His side, really going with Him to suffering and death as they had pledged themselves to do. How differently Peter would have acted when he was asked whether he was a follower of Christ. How different it would have been for the other Apostles. A little more prayer, a little more dedication to Christ could have made that difference.

There are many who have learned from the mistakes of the Apostles, and do keep their whole lives thus dedicated to Christ and His will. In Maura Laverty's story of Irish country life, *Never No More,* there is pictured a saintly old woman, praying to God at the end of a long and busy day. Here is how the author describes it: "It was lovely to watch Gran when she was speaking to God. There was so much there besides reverence. Such a brave confidence in the lift of the small withered chin. Such a trusting friendliness in the intimacy of her half-whispered words. When Gran knelt down to pray you could almost hear her saying; 'Are You by Yourself, Lord? Can I come in for a minute or two? I'm afraid I'm no great shakes of a visitor for You. Look at the state of me! I didn't get a minute all day to titivate my soul. But I thought I'd drop in anyway — You always give me such a welcome. There's a few things I wanted to talk over with You — maybe You'll tell me what to do about them. A couple of friends of mine are in a bit of trouble and, if it isn't asking too much, I'd like You to help them. And then there's a few odds and ends of my own I wanted to chat about. Look — here's how it is. . . .'

"She blessed herself and rose from her knees, murmuring as she always did when she had concluded her prayers, 'Not my will, O Lord, but Thine be done,' thereby signifying that if she had made any unreasonable or senseless requests she would not be offended if they were ignored, but would understand perfectly."

Few writers have expressed so well what praying to God should really mean — asking for things, common, ordinary, perhaps unimportant things, but wanting most of all that God's will be done. Memorized prayers have their place, often a necessary place in the worship of God, but there is a time when we instinctively turn from them to a direct, personal conversation with God. We speak to God as directly and feelingly as did the centurion who cried: "Say but the word and my servant shall be healed." We cry out to Him as desperately as did the Apostle Peter when he felt himself about to be engulfed by the waves of the Lake of Genesareth: "Lord, save us, we perish." We point out our needs to Him as specifically as did our Blessed Mother at the wedding feast of Cana when she reminded Him: "They have no wine." All of these motives and emotions enter into our prayers at times, but in each prayer there should be the attitude of submission to God's will, which Christ so perfectly expressed in His prayer in the Garden of Olives: "Lord, not my will but thine be done."

The main purpose of our prayers is not to have God do our will, but to bring our will into harmony with His, to accept and to accomplish what He desires. Christ taught us this in the Our Father: "Thy will be done on earth as it is in heaven." When the Apostles learned these words, they could not yet suspect the scope of their meaning. They could not imagine how hard it might be to repeat them with Christ in the Garden of Olives: "Not my will but thine be done." But neither had they learned the more comforting fact, that if in all the lesser things of life we accept God's will, there is nothing that can occur which will be too hard for us to endure.

# The Hidden Christ

DURING THE MIDDLE AGES, THERE WAS A legend that spread among many peoples and many lands. According to this story, a very remarkable incident occurred as our Lord carried His cross out to Calvary on the first Good Friday. Along the way that our Saviour traveled, there lived a cobbler. When Jesus arrived at the man's place of business, He was almost dead from pain and fatigue and thirst. He paused at the door of this man's shop, and humbly asked him for a cup of water to relieve His thirst. The cobbler did not recognize the Son of God in the torn and bleeding figure that stood before him. He saw a disgraced criminal being led out to execution. He saw unfavorable notice being drawn to himself and to his place of business. Perhaps he even feared what might be done if he should seem to be a friend of this Man. And so, he sharply refused the request of Christ. "Why dost Thou tarry here?" he asked Him, and commanded Him to pass on. Christ did as He was commanded. He continued on His way, but first He said to this unfeeling man: "I go away, but tarry thou upon the earth till I come again."

According to the legend, the years passed on and the cobbler grew old, but still he did not die. He became a wanderer upon the face of the earth, going from place to place, never finding either a home or rest. Every hundred years, his youth returns and he is young again, only to pass through the same cycle. In the course of all these centuries, this wanderer has learned all sorts of wisdom. Especially has he learned the lesson of human kindness and Christian charity. His life is now dedicated to bringing help to all those who need it, whether they be individuals or nations. He has seen all the tragedies of the world, and as he goes on his way, he bears a look of ineffable sadness.

That is only a legend, only a story of something that might have happened, but didn't. Or is it only that? Is it not basically a true story? Is it not in its main outline a version of something that has happened not once but a million times, something that is happening today? Perhaps Christ never asked for a cup of water personally, and was refused. But Christ has said: "Whatsoever you have done to the least of these, my brethren, you have done also to me." Countless brothers and sisters of Christ have needed so much, and asked for so much, and have been curtly told to be on their way. We may not see in this a refusal given to Christ, but that is how He regards it. And that is how a true Christian conscience should regard any offense against the charity that we owe to all of our fellow men.

In one of his less-known stories, *Door of Unrest*, O. Henry pictures a man who had offended against Christian charity, and who realized the real nature of his fault, but was thrown into a sort of despair because he did not know how to remedy it. He paints this man somewhat in the fashion of the old legend of the Wandering Jew.

He describes him as "old Father Time's younger brother. His face was beardless and as gnarled as an English walnut. I never saw clothes such as he wore. They would have reduced Joseph's coat to a monochrome. But the colors were not the dyer's. Stains and patches and the work of sun and rust were responsible for the diversity. On his coarse shoes was the dust, conceivably, of a thousand leagues. . . . I can describe him no further, except to say that he was little and weird and old — so old I began to estimate in centuries when I saw him. Yes, and I remember that there was an odor, a faint odor like aloes, or possibly like myrrh or leather."

The man's story, as he told it, was not unlike the medieval legend of the man who had commanded Christ to be on His way to Calvary. But, in the telling, it became evident that while the storyteller was sincere, he was not sober, and the man to whom the story was told decided to investigate. He finally unearthed the truth. The old man was named Mike O'Bader. His hallucination went back over a period of thirty years. As one of the old settlers of the town told the story: "Well, Mike O'Bader had a daughter then — a right pretty girl. She was too gay a sort for Montopolis, so one day she slips off to another town and runs away with a circus. It was two years before she comes back, all fixed up in fine clothes and rings and jewelry, to see Mike. He wouldn't have nothin' to do with her, so she stays around town awhile, anyway. I reckon the men folks wouldn't have raised no objections, but the women egged 'em on to order her to leave town. But she had plenty of spunk, and told 'em to mind their own business. So one night they decided to run her away. A crowd of men and women drove her out of her house, and chased her with sticks and stones. She run to her father's door, callin' for help. Mike opens it, and when he sees who it is he hits her with his fist and knocks her down and shuts the door. And then the crowd kept on chunkin' her till she run clear out of town. And the next day they finds her drowned dead in Hunter's mill pond. . . . When old Mike has a spell, he thinks he's the Wanderin' Jew. . . . 'He is,' said I, nodding away."

The obligation to practice charity toward our fellow men is not always drawn in such strong colors. The failure to live up to our obligation does not often have such tragic consequences. But, in lesser things, the story is re-enacted every day in almost every human life. "Whatsoever you have done for the least of these, my brethren, you have done also to me." Christ's command could not be more clear or specific. Nor could we have more cogent reasons for loving Him. All that we are, all that we have, all that is possible to us is due to His goodness. And beyond that, He has suffered and died to save us from our own folly. Certainly we owe Him very much, and certainly He has the right to specify the manner in which we shall try to pay our debt. If He chooses to require kindness to others, if He wishes to regard such kindness as kindness to Himself that is His right. And we can only regulate our attitude toward others accordingly.

There are offenses against charity in the life of everyone of us. We should recognize them as faults, as faults calling for correction. They should not drive us to drink or to despair as they did the man portrayed in O. Henry's story. They should drive us on to correct the result of past uncharitableness, and to avoid their repetition in the future. The Wandering Jew never existed except in the words of the old legend; but the mistake attributed to him will exist in your life and in mine unless we treat our fellow man as we would treat Christ Himself.

# Working for God

IN NEARLY EVERY HUMAN BEING, THERE IS A tendency to approve and applaud when anyone does good to his fellow man. There are some exceptions to this rule. There are people who are filled with envy or jealousy or hatred of others. But these exceptions are only exceptions.

However, the fact that we approve the good done by others, or at least do not oppose it, does not fulfill our duties or our possibilities. To some extent, at least, we are our brother's keeper, and we have the duty of bestirring ourself on his behalf. But only God was able to devise effective means of getting us to do so. The means He chose was His own personal example — the love for mankind which led Him to suffer and die for the redemption of the world.

There are many people who have admired the works of true Christian charity, and have tried to produce the same effects but with lesser motives. In the *Magnificent Obsession,* Lloyd Douglas portrays such an attempt. He describes several people trying to do good to everyone who might come their way, to the poor, to the sick, to the victims of injustice, and even to those who had caused the injustice. He pictures these people as making great personal sacrifices, spending their time and their money, hiding their good works except from those who had to know, and doing this not out of Christian charity, but because of a secret power and reward which would come to them whenever they did such actions. For example, the author pictures a man, whose ordinary occupation was putting letters on memorial stones, becoming a great sculptor as a reward for secretly doing good to others; a doctor of somewhat ordinary ability becoming a world-famous brain specialist by the same means; another doctor being enabled to invent a device to revolutionize the technique of surgery. There is portrayed here a natural counterpart of supernatural charity. There is great personal effort and sacrifice, but the goal is of such passing importance. It is to improve life only in this world and not the spiritual and eternal life of men and women. The motive for doing good to others is human success and not a desire to imitate and repay Him who "loved me and delivered himself up for me." It is charity, but it is not Christian charity.

There are undoubtedly people who make such great efforts for such transitory results. Their sacrifice may be, at times, heroic, and at times they see themselves as other Christs. As one of the characters in the *Magnificent Obsession* describes it: "If, however, you seriously wish to proceed, let me counsel you . . . that you are taking hold of high tension! Once you have touched it, you will never be able to let go. . . . If you are of the temperament that demands self-indulgence to keep you happy and confident enough to do your work . . . leave all this alone, and go your way. For if you make an excursion into this you're bound. It will plaster a mortgage on everything you think you own, and commandeer your time when you might prefer to be using it for yourself. It is very expensive. It took the man who discovered it to a cross at the age of thirty-three!"

With those few words, and without even introducing the name of Christ, the author tries to make his thoughts Christ's thoughts, his motives Christ's motives. The attempt cannot succeed. Christ was not merely a good man paying the supreme price for the earthly welfare of others. He was the God-Man procuring their eternal welfare.

In so many of the things that Christ did for the whole world, He not only did not seek publicity, but commanded that nothing be said. However, if we are familiar with all that He said and did, we can see that there was no mystery at all about His acting in this way. It is simply a matter of the reason for our charity toward others. If we are doing it in order to obtain praise, then that praise is itself the reward for any good that we do. It is like paying for an ad in a newspaper. The publicity itself is recompense for what we expend. If we are doing it, however, out of love for God and gratitude to God, then any commendation that we receive is superfluous and accidental. Christ stated this so clearly. "Do not your good works to be seen by men. Do them in secret for your Heavenly Father, and your Father who seeth in secret will reward you." Keeping our good works secret from men is prescribed so that we might not be tempted to do them for men instead of for God.

Christ loved us not for our own sakes, but because of our relationship with God. He saw so clearly that our real importance and our greatest worth consists not in the things we possess in this world, not in the pleasures we are able to enjoy here on earth, but rather in being friends of God and having the right to everlasting happiness with Him. That is what He wanted us to have. That was the reason for the teaching and example that He gave us. That was His purpose in suffering and dying. It was so important a goal, even in the sight of God, that it was worth the life and the death of Christ. Our Lord did feed the hungry, comfort the sorrowing, heal the sick, but these things were not the main purpose of His life and death. Christ came to lead the world back to the God who made it. The follower of Christ who really tries to follow Him is animated by the same spirit. There are countless things which we must do for people, countless ways in which we can make life in this world better and more livable. Our main purpose, like the main purpose of Christ, should be to bring others to know, to love, and to serve God. And because we are doing this in imitation of Christ and out of gratitude for what He has done for us, we do not look for thanks or appreciation from others. In fact, as far as possible, we should avoid the commendation of others, lest Christ's words concerning the Pharisees be applied to us: "I say to you, they have already received their reward."

If there were some secret power that would come to anyone who would do works of charity for others and keep those good works secret, that power would be well known and would be much used. Earthly fame and earthly success usually mean so much that many people would try anything, even charity toward others, if they could attain these results. Fortunately, such is not the case. If such rewards were to be had the temptation to do good for the sake of these tangible rewards would almost certainly kill charity and set up in its place unspeakable greed and self-seeking. The good which

God promises is less tangible, but very, very real. What Christ accomplished by His sufferings and death is the secret and the cause of all the works of Christian charity. Every act of true Christian charity, whether it be performed by some great saint or by some unknown and unsung follower of Christ, is the direct result of Christ's sufferings. All that you or I may do for the welfare of others, does not bring us any particular earthly fame, but it does bring our lives and the lives of others closer to God. The heroic self-sacrifice and generosity of young and old, of those dedicated to God by Baptism and those dedicated to Him by special vows, are often barren of any outstanding earthly rewards, but are not without great and lasting worth. They have been done for God, and He will reward them.

# Truly Sorry

AMONG ALL THE THINGS WHICH CHRIST OF-
fered to do for the world, scarcely anything created so much
opposition and contradiction as His offer to forgive sins. John
the Baptist had hailed our Lord as the "Lamb of God who
taketh away the sins of the world." That was not a new or
amazing title. In fact, it was the general expectation of
what the promised Messias would accomplish. But there
seemed to be a great difference between merely expecting a
vague someone who would forgive sins, and hearing Christ
whom they could see and hear say to an individual, "Go in
peace, thy sins are forgiven thee." Moreover, the opposition
which Christ encountered in this matter was not confined to
Himself alone. It extends to the Church He established
when it attempts to do the work He commissioned it to do.
"If they have persecuted me, they will persecute you." Down
through the Christian years, the Church has carried out the
command of Christ: "Whose sins you shall forgive, they are

forgiven; and whose sins you shall retain, they are retained." Almost invariably, there is contradiction if not bitter opposition.

Perhaps the basic reason why so many people cannot understand the forgiveness of sins, whether it be by Christ or by His Church, is the fact that they do not see the whole picture, do not see what is really required. To them, it seems that all that is necessary is that one admit his sins, and they are taken away, and they feel that it should not be as simple as that. As a matter of fact, it is not as simple as that. Mere recognition of one's faults, mere confession of them, is not sufficient to win forgiveness. That is why Christ left to His priests the power, sometimes to forgive and sometimes not to forgive. In the use of this power, they were not to be arbitrary or act according to their personal likes or prejudices. They are to give or withhold forgiveness of sins depending upon whether there is or is not true sorrow and repentance.

Christ, being God, knew people's dispositions without asking them. He did not impart forgiveness of sins to everyone He happened to meet, even though everyone could very well use God's forgiveness. He gave it when He saw it was necessary AND deserved, where there was true sorrow for having offended God. The priest, bringing God's forgiveness must usually proceed more slowly and circumspectly. When a man is in danger of death, and there is not time for inquiries or delay, absolution of sins is given with the hope that the dying person is able to profit by it, but at other times the priest must be as sure as he can be that the person is deserving of God's forgiveness and is properly disposed to accept it.

In *Weeping Cross,* a novel by Henry L. Stuart, the leading

character is a young man, who was sent out from England to Massachusetts during the early colonial days. He was sent not as a settler but as an indentured servant, who must work for whoever might take him and do whatever tasks might be assigned to him. There was no opportunity for the young man to practice his religion. He was an alien, in nationality and religion, set among a people who hated and despised and feared him. The daughter of the man who hired him gradually felt herself attracted to him, and while at first she despised his servile condition too much to consider marriage, she accepted him as her lover. Finally, a rescue party arrived to lead him to freedom, and this woman agreed to go with him and become his wife. There were priests in the rescue party, and the young man's first concern was to be validly married. First, he must go to confession to obtain forgiveness of his sins, and there in the wilderness he kneels and candidly admits his offenses against God. However, the priest can find little evidence that he is truly sorry for his sins, and the young man describes what followed. He asks the priest: " 'Were I dying you would absolve me, can ye not do the like now?' 'Ah, Richard,' says my old master sadly, 'death presents no problem, but solves them all; 'tis when we priests deal with life that we tremble at the responsibility God puts in our hand.' His lips moved awhile in prayer; then tossing his head a little, as one that giveth sign he hears a message aright, he bent over me a face whereon was the reflex of God's eternal love and indulgence. 'You shall have absolution,' says he, 'but upon a condition; without it I dare not spend the blood of Christ for you.' 'Name it,' says I eagerly, yet my heart quaked too. 'If I bid you in God's name, send this woman away, and come with us, will ye do it?' There was a moment of struggle, and then submission. 'Father,' said I, wearily, 'whatever you command me that I will do, but would God I had died today before 't was asked of me.' To which, the priest replied, ' 'Tis well. I will absolve you and marry you too.' "

What that particular priest required in that particular case as evidence of true repentance for sin, is a somewhat incidental thing. The important fact is that he realized, as the Church insists, that forgiveness for sin cannot be given unless a man is willing to receive it, unless he is truly sorry for the sins that have made him need forgiveness. That is the condition. As the priest says in this fictional incident: "without it I dare not spend the blood of Christ for you."

The blood of Christ was shed for the remission of men's sins, for the redemption of the world. It accomplishes its purpose through the Sacraments, and chiefly through the Sacrament of Penance. In particular cases, it may produce its effect even outside the Sacraments, as it does when a person is truly sorry for his sins and cannot receive the Sacrament of Penance, but makes an act of perfect contrition. No matter how or where or when, Christ's sufferings forgive our sins, they can do so only if we are sorry for what we have done. If we remember and understand this always, we who use the Sacrament of Penance will always use it well; those who do not make use of it, will at least not disparage it. All will be forced to marvel at God's love which allows His ministers "to spend the blood of Christ for you."

# The Last Chance

IT IS A COMMONLY ACCEPTED FACT THAT PEO-
ple do not usually become suddenly good or bad. Whether
a man heads upward or downward, he usually follows a
path. In going upward, he does not fly; in going downward
he does not fall over a precipice. It is all step by step in
the same direction. That is why people are so skeptical
about sudden conversions or unexpected revelations of evil.
If a man is caught doing wrong, the first suspicion is that
he has been that way all along — and has just gotten caught.
If he suddenly appears as much better than he has been,
they wonder what new fraud he has devised.

That is the ordinary run of things, but there are exceptions. A man can toil to the top of a mountain, and turn
aside just short of his goal; and, on the other hand, he
can decend almost to the bottom, then turn and go back.
In natural things, it is simply a matter of choice. In spiritual
things, it is a matter of choice plus God's grace. And some-

times God's grace can be so powerful that the human will does things it never expected to do.

Evelyn Waugh records such an instance. In *Brideshead Revisited,* he presents Lord Marchmain who was a Catholic, at least in name. This man spent the latter years of his life living with a woman who was not his wife. The commands of God seemed to mean nothing to him, and he faced the approach of death without any particular repentance or regret. In fact, on one occasion when he seemed to be in extreme danger, a priest was summoned and he refused even to see him.

With this background, any last-minute penitence would seem unlikely. It would be unlikely, but it can happen, and sometimes does happen. The deathbed scene of this man is described by an onlooker who was a man of no religious faith. "The priest bent over Lord Marchmain and blessed him. . . . 'Now,' said the priest, 'I know you are sorry for all the sins of your life, aren't you? Make a sign, if you can. You're sorry, aren't you?' But there was no sign. 'Try and remember your sins; tell God you are sorry. I am going to give you absolution. While I am giving it, tell God you are sorry you have offended Him.' He began to speak in Latin. I recognized the words Ego te absolvo in nomine Patris . . . and saw the priest make the sign of the cross. Then I knelt, too, and prayed: 'O God, if there is a God, forgive him his sins, if there is such a thing as sin,' and the man on the bed opened his eyes and gave a sigh, the sort of sigh I had imagined people made at the moment of death, but his eyes moved so that we knew there was still life in him.

"I suddenly felt the longing for a sign, if only a courtesy, if only for the sake of the woman I loved, who knelt in front of me, praying, I knew, for a sign. It seemed so small a thing that was asked, the bare acknowledgment of a present, a nod in the crowd. All over the world people were on their knees before innumerable crosses, and here the drama was being played again by two men — by one man, rather, and he nearer death than life; the universal drama in which there is only one actor.

"The priest took the little silver box from his pocket and spoke again in Latin, touching the dying man with an oily wad; he finished what he had to do, put away the box and gave the final blessing. Suddenly Lord Marchmain moved his hand to his forehead; I thought he had felt the touch of the chrism and was wiping it away. 'O God,' I prayed, 'Don't let him do that.' But there was no need for fear; the hand moved slowly down his breast, then to his shoulder, and Lord Marchmain made the sign of the cross. Then I knew that the sign I had asked for was not a little thing, not a passing nod of recognition, and a phrase came back to me from my childhood of the veil of the temple being rent from top to bottom."

The last-minute repentance that came to that dying man, the acceptance of the last grace in life after rejecting all the graces that had gone before, is certainly contrary to all the laws of likelihood or probability. Usually, it is true that as a man lives, so shall he die. A man can get into such a habit of casting aside God and all that God would do for him that eventually he does this automatically with scarcely any realization of what it is that he is rejecting. He can seem beyond the reach of any words and of every argument. But God's grace still cries out importunately for admission into his life, and it is never too late for it to work.

The ordinary works that a man can accomplish in life require both time and effort. If they are neglected beyond a certain stage in life, they are neglected completely and forever. But in the most important work of any man's life — turning from sin and turning to God — it is never too late so long as life endures. In this, man's work consists for the most part of allowing God to work within him, and God's works are accomplished perfectly and in an instant. In the beginning of the world, God had only to command the creation of sun and moon and earth, and even of man himself, and promptly they sprang into existence. God's word was spoken, and they were there. God's power in the spiritual order is no less infinite, but He will not use that power without our consent. Christ, on the cross, was just as eager to convert the criminal on His left as He was to win over the thief on His right. His divine grace hovered equally over each. But one admitted it, and was turned into a saint; the other died unrepentant.

There is encouragement in this for all of us. While we have life, it is never too late to repent of our mistakes. The important thing, however, is the fact that the only moment of life of which we are certain, is this one present moment. We are promised nothing in the future, we can be sure only of the opportunity we have here and now. And God Himself has emphasized this over and over. "Now is the acceptable time, now is the day of salvation." "Today, if you shall hear His voice, harden not your hearts." At the last moment of life, the man described by Evelyn Waugh deliberately made the sign of the cross and allowed the power of the Cross to transform his soul. He had postponed the moment of repentance many, many times. If he had postponed it just once more, that moment never would have come.

# The Bitter Cup

SOME MONTHS AGO, THE MOTHER OF A LITTLE
girl of two years was teaching her daughter a few simple
religious practices. She had taught the child how to make
the sign of the cross, how to say grace before meals, how to
say a few short prayers before going to bed at night. The
child was very interested, and one day she surprised her
mother by asking her about the crucifix that hung above
her bed. "What was it?" "Who was it?" "How did it happen?"
The mother tried to explain in very simple words that God,
to whom she prayed every day, had become Man, and that
He had been nailed to the cross. That satisfied the child's
curiosity for the time being, and the mother thought that
she had forgotten all about it. After a few days, the little
girl came back with another question. She asked, "Mother,
do I have to be nailed to the cross like God was?"

It is futile for any adult to try to follow the processes of
a child's mind. A child's reasoning or chain of thought is

considerably different from our own. Somehow or other, in her own mind and in her own way that little girl arrived at this definite conclusion: "If God suffered, then it is quite reasonable to expect that we too might have to suffer." She would not have expressed it like that, but that was certainly the meaning of her question. She had hit upon the truth expressed in St. Peter's epistle: "Christ suffered for us, leaving you an example that you should follow in his footsteps."

The necessity of suffering is certainly not a welcome truth for anyone of us. Some of the saints attained to a state where they desired suffering, but that is far from the ordinary desire. In fact, far from desiring it, many people find it their greatest difficulty to reconcile themselves to it. Many are filled with doubt or wonderment or resentment merely to find that God permits suffering to exist in the world and in the lives of other people. It is not surprising that their emotions are much stronger when they find suffering approaching their own lives. Sometimes they find sight or hearing or some other faculty seriously impaired or destroyed; again it may be some wasting disease that reduces them to an existence of inactivity or of pain; or again it may be an accident that suddenly destroys all their dreams of the future, leaving little of the joys of living. In a thousand different ways, in great things and in trifles, we are all very vulnerable, and sometimes when we least expect it, the burden of suffering takes up a permanent place in our life. And whether we welcome it or tolerate it or fight it, there is no escape.

The sufferings of Christ offered to the world an escape from futile and useless suffering, but not an escape from suffering itself. They present a pattern which anyone can learn to apply to whatever sufferings may come into his life.

Owen Francis Dudley faces this problem of accepting

suffering in his novel *Shadow on the Earth*. He presents the story of a young man who is hopelessly crippled for life while climbing in the Alps.

As the first shock of the accident wears off, "He began to think. He began to think deliberately, fiercely. He thought of all that life had meant to him: of his undergraduate days, of his games, his triumphs, of the cups standing on his mantelpiece at home. He saw them standing there now — in mockery. He saw the colors of the county he played for, hanging in his cupboard. His mind travelled to the stables; he was patting the silky neck of his favourite mount; swinging himself into the saddle. Then to the garage — his car. He was on the road — switching her on to the full; trees and hedges whistling by. Then his friends — his endless friends; bridge friends, tennis friends; those summer days on the courts — tea inside. He could hear the great Georgian house, his home, ringing with their laughter. He saw the sunny lawns in front sloping down to the cool of the trees and river. He was swimming in the clear depths, diving into them off the bank, shouting to the others stripping there, shouting for sheer joy of life. Great nights in London flashed before him. . . . Dinner, wild dinners . . . mad pranks. . . . Afterwards the show . . . the sensuous rhythm of the jazz band. Faces came back to him; faces of the women he had danced with, fooled; faces of the women he had loved. . . . Yes, that was life; gorgeous, full-blooded life!

"Suddenly he came back to realities — to what had happened. The horror of it returned — redoubled. Sweat broke out on his forehead."

He was a helpless cripple, with no possibility of ever being anything but that. The swing of the pendulum had been complete — only there would be no return. He had enjoyed every pleasure that life had to offer, and now he had none of them. Enjoyment had been his life, his all; now that it was gone, there seemed to be nothing at all that was left. Up to that moment, this man had spoken glibly of the havoc of human suffering; he had agreed wholeheartedly that the suffering men and women who were beyond the reach of medical cure should be gently exterminated, as one would destroy a suffering animal. It was only when suffering had touched him personally that he began to seek whether there might not be some escape from despair. He was fortunate enough to find what he sought.

Bit by bit, the meaning of Christ's suffering became clear to that crippled young man. At first, it seemed fantastic, too good to be true. At first, there were only the unfamiliar almost meaningless words. But then, his own sufferings brought an understanding of the sufferings of Christ. Christ on the cross became Someone close to him, Someone very real to him, Someone all-important to him. He pondered ever more deeply the mystery of the Son of God suffering for sin, dying for the salvation of the world, atoning for his sins. When his mind turned from that to a consideration of his own sufferings, these were no longer the greatest, most important things in his life. They were incidental, insignificant, nothing in comparison with what Christ had endured so willingly. Suddenly he found that his rebellion against God, his bitterness at his sufferings, was gone. He had lost very much, but he had not lost anything that really mattered. In fact, he had gained far more than he had lost. He had lost a certain amount of pleasures which no one could have for more than a short time at most; he had gained God, whom he could keep forever.

Finally, he was granted an understanding or a vision of

the final goal of all Christian suffering. He saw Christ, "Who had hung upon a Cross, the King of heaven and earth, Creator of all that is — the God Who was crucified by His creatures, Who gave His life to save — His hands and feet and side a blaze of glorious wounds. . . ." With Christ were His saints who had suffered with and for Him.

Such was the vision granted to that cripple; such is the hope offered to each of us; such is the promise made by God Himself, who tells us: "If we have suffered with Him, we shall also be glorified with Him."

# The Unending Problem

DURING THE LATTER DAYS OF WORLD WAR II, there was a very commonly used expression: "They were expendable." It was a simple statement of a belief that one man might well be expected to die for a group of men, or that the general welfare came before the welfare of the few. If an army must be withdrawn from some untenable position, a few men might be left as rear guard with almost the certainty that their death would be the price of the life of others. If essential information had to be obtained even at the cost of very great risk, the value to the common good was felt to justify the death of those who might have to obtain that information. In wartime, no one could publicly question the right of the state to require men to sacrifice themselves for the welfare of their fellow men. Even in times of less urgency, most people will agree with the principle. It is not a new principle. Nineteen hundred years ago, it was taken for granted. Caiphas, the high priest, used the principle to justify the destruction of Christ. "It is expedient for one man to die so that the whole nation might not perish."

When a man or group of men are called to die for their fellow men, usually they do not even know just why this sacrifice is being required of them. The plans of a high command seldom trickle down to the army rear guard. Much less can anyone question the wisdom of such plans. At times the plans themselves may be wise; at other times, they may be folly. Sometimes, the sacrifice made will be worth while and effective; at other times, it will be in vain. In either case, one scarcely feels that anyone has the right to be critical.

If we admit the right of the state to decide that certain human lives are expendable, it is quite as logical, and even much more so, to recognize the right of God to decide when human lives are expendable. Human life does not belong to the state in the same way in which it belongs to God. The state merely has certain rights over human life. It does not give that life. It does not have supreme rights over it. God IS the Author of all life. God has the unlimited right to confer life and to take it away. Moreover, when God does confer the gift of life, He does not give it for any specified time. He does not say to anyone: "You will have fifty or sixty or seventy years of life." He gives life to His human creatures without any commitments or stipulations whatsoever. He reserves to Himself the right to give life and to take it away. He acts like the owner of the vineyard described in our Lord's parable — the employer who paid everyone what was just, and gave most of his workers much that they did not deserve. If God gives a single instant of life to any of us, it is something that we did not have a strict right to receive. Much more so is every additional moment of life a free gift from God. If we are blessed with long life, we have no right

[ 76 ]

to criticize God because He has not made our life still longer or because He has not given the same gift to everyone. If God's plans call for one person to live many years while someone else hardly gets acquainted with life, God has a right to carry out His plans. We have no rights against God. We are all entirely expendable, when it is a matter of carrying out the things which God has planned according to His infinite wisdom.

All of us who have any fundamental understanding of our religion know this, and admit this. But when we see it actually applied to human life, it is sometimes hard for us to acquiesce. Often we see people of evil life continue on and on. Then, on the other hand, we see so many necessary and good people die. We bow to the infinite wisdom of God, we submit to the will of God. It is not always easy. It is so natural to ask: "Why?" And so often, God does not answer that question.

In the popular novel *How Green Was My Valley*, Richard Llewellyn broaches this problem. He brings it up with reference to a little girl who had been brutally murdered. The girl's father, Mr. Pritchard, asks his minister for an explanation. Here is his reply: " 'I cannot tell you, Mr. Pritchard, my little one,' Mr. Gruffydd said, and his voice deep and full of sorrow, and bringing the room to quiet. 'No man can tell you. I could say that she was taken as a punishment, or as a visitation. But what have you done? Or your good wife? And if you were to be punished, why your little girl and not you? No, Mr. Pritchard. I cannot answer you, for nothing I could say would be the truth. The truth is beyond us, and is not in us. We go forward in faith. That is all.' 'Yes,' said Mr. Pritchard. 'I suppose so, indeed. But it is very hard.' 'Nobody can tell why the Son of Man had to go,' Mr. Gruffydd said. 'He was Prince of Light. He could have ruled the world. But He was crucified, and when men would have fought for Him, He told them to put up their swords. He allowed a rabble to crucify Him. Why did He die in that way when He could have chosen any? To save us, we know. But why did He die in only that way? It was ordained?' "

God does not answer all our questions. The very nature of our condition in this world, the thing that makes our life in this world meritorious for us, is the fact that we do take things on faith. Christ summed it up so succinctly. "Blessed are they who have not seen, and have believed." If the death of the Son of God upon the cross is beyond our comprehension, it is reasonable that merely human deaths should not be perfectly explainable. God, who is infinite goodness, could allow His Son to die. He is no less good when He allows death to strike close to us. The death of Christ and all human deaths are equally a part of God's plans. If the life of Christ was expendable, so are all human lives. We must realize, however, that what is expended is not wasted. Christ's death was futile in the eyes of many, but God was using it as the means of redeeming the world. So, too, our frustrations, our sufferings, our death — when and how these may occur — are permitted by God or willed by God for purposes that are divine.

# The Alchemy of Life

DURING RECENT YEARS, SCIENTISTS HAVE concerned themselves with many problems which had previously seemed to offer them little chance of success. They have, for example, tried to analyze and measure the extent of human pain. They have devised measuring instruments and technical terms to interpret their meaning. They have uncovered some facts which seem to be new, and they have found scientific proof for some things which everyone believed all along. They have discovered that there is a threshold where pain begins and also a limit to human suffering, an extreme of pain which cannot be exceeded. They have found that one pain can supersede another, so that the former is not even adverted to in the face of the greater and more recent pain.

This last conclusion, which seems so surprising, is not really new at all. It was discovered long ago that athletes in the excitement of a contest, have often been hardly conscious of serious injuries and pain. Soldiers, in the midst of battle, are often blissfully unaware of wounds they have suffered. We find like evidence also in the realm of religious experience. Many of the saints have been totally unconscious of bodily pain while they were totally preoccupied with religious mysteries; and even lesser Christians have been able to experience something quite similar. A spirit of zealous dedication to religious tasks can cause bodily aches and pains to recede insignificantly into the background. Concentration on religious truths cannot reasonably be put forward as a remedy for bodily sufferings, yet it does often quite effectively fulfill that purpose.

Something of this is suggested in *Death Comes for the Archbishop* by Willa Cather. The missionary bishop, Jean Marie Latour, loses his way on one of his trips across his vast western diocese.

"He had no water left in his canteen, and the horses had had none since yesterday morning. They had made a dry camp in these hills last night. The animals were almost at the end of their endurance, but they would not recuperate until they got water, and it seemed best to spend their last strength in searching for it. On a long caravan trip across Texas, this man had had some experience of thirst, as the party with which he travelled was several times put on a meagre water ration for days together. But he had not suffered then as he did now. Since morning he had had a feeling of illness; the taste of fever in his mouth, and alarming seizures of vertigo. As these conical hills pressed closer and closer upon him, he began to wonder whether his long wayfaring from the mountains of Auvergne were possibly to end here. He reminded himself of that cry, wrung from his Saviour on the Cross, 'J'ai soif' (I thirst). Of all our Lord's physical sufferings, only one, 'I thirst,' rose to His lips. Empowered

[ 80 ]

by long training the young priest blotted himself out of his own consciousness and meditated upon the anguish of his Lord. The Passion of Jesus became for him the only reality; the need of his own body was but a part of that conception."

What that man experienced in the pages of fiction, countless Christians have experienced in real life. On the sickbed and on the deathbed, the crucifix, the remembrance of Christ's sufferings, has brought strength and hope to the spirit, but it has brought no less alleviation to the body. Even the less tangible pains of human life — the slights, the insults, the disappointments of life — all these have so often found their relief in the sight and remembrance of Christ's sufferings. Before this is possible, however, Christ must mean very much to us, He must be very personal, and His sufferings very real to us. The ordinary person of any sensibilities is disturbed by an account of human misery or suffering, but even the acute distress and misery of people whom he has never seen, and never expects to see, will usually not mean as much to him as the slightest injury or suffering of someone near and dear to him. Doctors and nurses, for example, come in daily contact with all degrees of human misery; they seldom become impervious to all human pain. They may acquire a professional or impersonal attitude about the sufferings of their patients, but their own sufferings and those of their relatives and friends still pierce sharply into their deeper feelings. Similarly, what the sufferings of Christ mean to us, and also what they do for us, depends upon what Christ Himself means to us, how close He is to us. If He is merely a historical person about whom we know some details, or if He is someone with whom we are barely on speaking terms, His sufferings cannot mean very much to us, much less can they ever supplant the consciousness of our own sufferings.

Christ's sufferings have supplied the fortitude and the spirit of endurance which Christianity has manifested so strikingly all down the years. The Christian man, woman, or child is no different from anyone else in his or her ordinary and natural reaction to the unpleasant and the painful. The afflictions of body and soul and mind press as heavily upon us as they do upon any human creature. When these afflictions come to us not from necessity but from the deliberate purpose of those who hate and persecute us, our first and instinctive reaction is one of rebellion and revenge. If these feelings have been quelled, if these emotions have been controlled, if Christians have been able to bear persecution down through all the ages, the credit is not due entirely to themselves. It is largely because the sharp edge of suffering has been dulled by a remembrance of the sufferings of Christ. The Apostles who fled in terror at the very thought of being involved with Christ in the hands of His enemies were the same men who later willingly submitted themselves to torture and death when the example of Christ's sufferings had penetrated deeply enough into their minds and hearts. Before this, they could say: "Lord, I will go with Thee unto suffering and unto death." Afterward, they found themselves able to keep that promise.

An understanding and appreciation of Christ's sufferings, therefore, is something that brings its reward even from a natural point of view. It will keep our spiritual life intact, but it will also bring an overflow of strength and courage and endurance into the vicissitudes and hardships of everyday living.

# My Brother's Keeper

SOMEONE HAS PROPOSED THE THEORY THAT
in the world of sports there are no upsets and there is little
that is unpredictable. He maintains that in any athletic
contest the results would always appear clearly in advance
if one knew accurately the ability, the training, and the
morale of the opposing persons or teams. Whatever may be
the merits of this theory in the realm of athletics, it is certainly a sound theory in the affairs of everyday life. Results
do not spring from chance or from fate. We reap what we
have sown. Circumstances may help or hinder us, but our
success or failure hinges rather upon what we are, how well
we know how to approach life's problems, and what use we
make of that knowledge. Our Christian religion provides for
us in all of these needs. It gives us an understanding of true
success, and it reveals methods of attaining success of which
we would never have conceived.

One of the specifically Christian means of accomplishing

things is by suffering. The more obvious and usually the easier way of doing things is by words or by actions, and these are good and effective means. Christ came into this world and dedicated three years to the work of preaching and doing good for others. His preaching was such that everyone was forced to admit: "Never did anyone speak as this Man speaks." The summary of His miracles corresponded to the gamut of human miseries and sufferings. Moreover, Christ instructed His Apostles to go forth to teach and to baptize and to do good to all, to relieve the maladies of soul and of body. Christ was certainly far from underestimating the value and importance of teaching and of good works. But when He came to His greatest task, the redemption of the world, He chose a new and different instrument of good. He redeemed mankind not by words of eloquence or wisdom but by silent, humble suffering; not by actions that filled all with wonder and amazement, but by enduring the suffering and death that His enemies inflicted upon Him.

Our sufferings do not have the same worth and efficacy as did the sufferings of Christ. He is the true Son of God; we are merely God's creations; but while our sufferings for others are not of infinite worth, their value should not be underestimated. They are often efficacious where our words and works are unavailing. That is why, for example, we have the age-old saying: "The blood of martyrs is the seed of Christians." One would expect that the appeal to reason or the example of Christian living would be the strongest appeal that one could make to a pagan mind. Experience, however, has shown so often that there is something still more effective. When Christian missionaries or people have suffered or died for the faith, there nearly always follows a vigor and a growth that nothing but the fact of suffering can adequately explain.

In the novel *Mirror for Toby*, Cecily Hallack has a priest explain something of this to one of the characters who is a rather worldly-minded Catholic. " 'It is curious,' mused Father Elstree, 'that we should be permitted by Almighty God to partake even of our Lord's work of redemption. Yet there it is: a necessary conclusion of the Incarnation. . . . If we are members of His body — the Lamb slain — insofar as we suffer obediently and in union with His will, we are part of Him Who works out the salvation of the whole world. Christ being dead, dieth now no more. But in us, in His mystical body, He is able to suffer and work by means of His members. We are cooperating with Him as the hands and feet cooperate with the brain. And sometimes we suffer for those we love, but it is His love that constrains us to do so, and His strength by which we persevere. And sometimes it is for those who are totally unknown to us, or those who are our enemies, or to whom we never give a thought. But our Lord loves them, and is mindful of them, is he not? Even when they ignore Him. He desires that they too should be brought to Him, and as St. Paul says: "We in our body make up the sufferings of Christ," because we are part of Him. But it is wonderful . . . to suffer for those dear to us. It is a very great happiness.' "

The idea of accomplishing something for others by suffering for them should be one of the most familiar of ideas, but it can often seem strange and repellent, unless we understand its real purpose. The father of a family who spends a long, hard day at exhausting labor is certainly not doing this for the pleasure it brings him, but rather for what his endurance and his efforts will bring to his family. The mother who denies herself so many things she would enjoy having, merely that her children might have more, is certainly not denying herself for the mere fun of doing so. She is accomplishing something which she feels is worth while. So, too, we do not seek suffering for its own sake or welcome it because of some secret charm we find in it. To do this, would be the perversion of all our natural instincts. We can welcome suffering because our faith has given us an insight into its possibilities, and we know that while suffering is sometimes futile it is not necessarily so. It can merit so much for ourselves and for others.

The idea of offering up to God, for others, the necessary and also the unnecessary sufferings and hardships of life has pretty well permeated the Christian consciousness. We are all familiar with the idea of making sacrifices for the missions and for the spread of the faith as well as making sacrifices to obtain God's special blessing upon those near to us. Sometimes, we may almost see the results of these sacrifices; at other times, the sacrifices we offer up for others may seem to be fruitless and unavailing. Of one thing, however, we can be certain. Just as no prayer of ours is ever wasted, just as God will always grant what is asked of Him or else grant something which He sees is better, so too our sacrifices for others, though for some reason failing to accomplish what we intended, will be directed to obtain the greater glory of God, which is really what we desire most. Hence, it is important never to lose the realization of the worth of sufferings offered up to God. It is our privilege to make the offering. It is God's part to apply our offering to the best advantage.

# The Mother's Place

DURING THE MANY CENTURIES BEFORE THE coming of Christ, God found it necessary to impose many restrictions upon the human race. He found, for example, that His people were very prone to fall into idolatry, and that He must safeguard them against this weakness. In fact, on the one occasion when God allowed the Israelites to set up an image for veneration, it was not long before they were actually worshiping it. The Brazen Serpent, which was the means God provided to free the people from the plague of the fiery serpents, finally had to be destroyed because it was being treated as an idol.

During the years that have passed since our Lord's time, the danger of idolatry has not been the same. Christianity has left its imprint upon the world. It has made known so much about God and the things of God that it is almost impossible for the old evil of idolatry to reassert itself. That is why from the earliest Christian era, representations of

Christ and of the saints have not only been allowed but encouraged. Christian men and women have always found it easier to remember Christ and what He did for us, to remember the saints and the example they gave to us, when they could see before themselves a representation of what others had visibly seen.

Artists of every degree have been almost as eager to represent Christ's Mother as they have been to portray our Lord Himself. They have realized how necessary it is for all of us to do what Christ commanded from the cross: "Son, behold thy Mother." And they have preferred to represent her as she was when Christ spoke those words, at the side of her Son on Calvary, heartbroken at the thought of His sufferings and His rejection by His people, but loving Him with unfaltering loyalty to the very end. Mary, the Sorrowful Mother, has been the favorite theme of artists, who have seen so much more than their brush or chisel or pen could ever represent. No one but God can tell how much this has done to keep a knowledge of Mary and a love for her alive in the world. No one can tell how much this has done to make it possible for Mary to fulfill her perpetual task of bringing mankind ever closer to her Son.

Like all good works, however, this too has met with contradiction and opposition. Periodically, there have arisen those who would destroy all earthly representations of Christ and of His saints. Strangely enough, devotion to Mary has been attacked with unreasoning hatred not only by those who would turn people away from God, but even by those who claimed to be leading them to God. They forgot that there is a world of difference between one who would come between us and God, and one who would lead us to God. Mary could never do anything but bring us to God. She is not God's rival. She is His Mother. She carries on her task despite all the foolish fears and unreasonable reasonings of those who have hated and attacked her. In fact, those who have fought against her, honestly though mistakenly, have often received the grace to realize their mistake, and come to a true understanding of God's Mother and theirs.

In the novel *Jesse and Maria,* by Enrica von Handel-Mazzetti, there is presented this struggle and this outcome. There is pictured an incident in the life of a little town in Austria. The people present the familiar cross section of Christian life, the very devout, the average, and the lukewarm. Upon a mountain, outside the town, there is a painting of the Sorrowful Mother, done by one of the townspeople, and placed by another in a shrine, as a token of his appreciation for a cure he received when praying before this picture. It was not a great work of art. It was not particularly beautiful even before time and the elements had ravaged it, but it did bring the Sorrowful Mother of Christ into all the sorrows of their life. There is in the town a man named Jesse, who resents this picture and all for which it stands. He is devoted to Christ, but he cannot see our Lady's place in Christianity, the place that Christ Himself has assigned to her. He dedicates himself to the destruction of this picture and its influence over the hearts and lives of these people. His efforts lead him to violence, and finally he is sentenced to death. In his death cell, in the last hours of his life, understanding finally comes to him.

"Jesse lifted his thin chained hands in the moonlight and looked at them. Once, he knew it well, he had been the most comely of knights. Women flushed with love if he even so much as glanced at them. Now, however, he was only a shadow of what he had been, and tomorrow he would be a grewsome thing; and yet if his darling were able she would kneel and kiss the bloody remains of his body . . . for she would not see death but only her beloved. And he realized that in quite the same way the love of a poor man, of a poor people, had made of that ugly painting something amiable and sweet, the symbol of the dear mother of Heaven — just as his own poor little cross was a sign of the dying Redeemer. If the guards were to come now and tear this cross from his hands, he would fight them like a lion. And the woman had defended the sacred treasure of her people, too, she had justly done so.

" 'It comforts us, sir,' she had said in her musical voice. 'When my baby died, it consoled me.' And what ought to be done to a man who tried to wound the souls of poor, burdened, hapless folk by taking from them their happiness and their source of refuge in need? Jesse sank on his knees beside the stone, laid his head on it — the head which in a few hours more would be severed from the body — struck his breast and whispered, 'I am a sinner.' "

Devotion to the Sorrowful Mother is really a form of devotion to the sufferings of Christ. Mary's sufferings were a part of the Passion. "There stood by the cross of Jesus, Mary his Mother." Those who were present on Calvary did not see Christ alone. Mary was a very definite, and very important, part of that picture. The sorrows of Mary find their meaning, their value, their importance only in their relation to the sufferings of Christ. She is the evidence that God did not intend to remove all suffering from the world; she is the proof that God can permit suffering to come even to His dearest friends; she is the example of the strength that God gives to those who suffer with Him and out of love for Him.

That is why the remembrance of the Sorrowful Virgin

has never grown dim in the minds of Christians. That is why every effort has been made that it shall never be forgotten. In fact, God Himself has encouraged the creation of pictures and statues of His Sorrowful Mother. He has done this by working miracles in places where some of these pictures and statues have been venerated. If, in spite of this, men see evil where God sees good, they are not seeing what God sees. They see some caricature which their distorted fancies have produced. They do not see the all-perfect Mother of Christ.

# Final Cleansing

EVERYONE WHO PROFESSES THE CHRISTIAN faith has some belief or other in heaven. Just what that belief is, just how clear it is, and just what it requires of them may show some variation. Yet, they do at least agree that there is such a place as heaven, that it is a place of unending happiness, and that it requires a certain minimum of effort and of goodness if one is to get there.

The Church tells with absolute certainty some of those who are in heaven — Christ, His Blessed Mother, and all the canonized saints. Over and above these, whom we may know by name, there is a vast multitude "of every tribe and every nation, whom no man can number." Further, the Church teaches, with the authority of God, that nothing defiled by sin, and that no one who is still obliged by the punishment due to sin, can enter heaven. These are very exacting requirements, but the Church offers us generously the means to fulfill them. The merits of the Passion of Christ applied to us in the Sacrament of Penance take away the guilt of sin and the eternal punishment due to it. Those same merits applied to us in the Sacrament of Extreme Unction take away the last vestiges of unworthiness that remain, and prepare us for the everlasting presence of God.

There are many people who are convinced of the importance and need of what we call the Last Sacraments as a preparation for death, but they do not understand exactly why they are so necessary. Shane Leslie, in *Doomsland*, pictures the Last Sacraments with rare understanding and discernment. His story describes a married woman who leaves her husband and runs away with a man with whom she has fallen in love. Her lover is somewhat surprised to hear her remark rather philosophically: " 'We have both given up a good deal for each other, haven't we, Edward?' 'You don't mean to say it was anything to give up that barrel of a fellow?' 'No, Edward, I should have left him anyhow, but I am giving up more than you dream.' 'You would never have got a penny from Clontibret, you know.' 'It's not that, Edward, but I have given my soul to be with you.' 'What do you mean? I always felt I could lose my soul to get you, and now I have got you, I don't care whether I have a soul left or not.' 'Well, Edward, I do care, for I really gave mine. I am a Catholic.' "

Here was a woman coolly and deliberately breaking the laws of God, giving up one thing in exchange for another, turning aside from God's law, God's friendship, choosing to lose her own soul in order that she might enjoy the love of one of God's creatures, a love which could not lawfully be hers. It was no rash or unpremeditated action, but a careful weighing of one thing against another, and making a free choice between them. Love and passion did enter into the matter, and did affect the decision, but they did not make it impossible to say no. They only made it more difficult.

Certainly this woman's disposition of mind made her unworthy to enter God's presence in heaven. It would be harder for an enemy of God to live in heaven than it would be to live in hell. In Mr. Leslie's story, however, that woman was given a chance to change her mind and her attitude toward God. She was given the opportunity to recognize her mistake, and to repent of her bargain. A bishop, who had been asked to give what help he could, came to that woman in her last sickness and helped prepare her for death. He heard her confession and imparted God's forgiveness. Then, as death approached more closely, he imparted the cleansing graces of Extreme Unction. As the author describes it: "The Bishop dipped his thumb in the Holy Oil and oiled the Sign of the Cross on her eyelids, saying: 'Per istam sanctam unctionem et suam piissimam misericordiam indulgeat tibi Dominus quidquid per visum deliquisti' ('Through this holy anointing and through His most gracious mercy, may the Lord forgive you whatever you have done to offend through sight'). With a morsel of wool he wiped the oil away and with it all the sins of the eye, her love of beauty and her memory of earth's coloured web, the vision of love, of himself, thought Edward. Never again would he see himself reflected in those violet balls. . . . 'Per istam sanctam unctionem' ('Through this holy anointing and through His most gracious mercy may the Lord forgive you whatever you have done to offend through hearing'). The divine indulgence was accorded to her ears, all she had ever heard wrong; all the wicked whispering of her lover was wiped away. By those fragile doors Edward felt he had entered into her life. And now the relentless Bishop had cleansed and sealed the porch, and the door was closed forever. . . . ('. . . may the Lord forgive you whatever you have done to offend through touch.') The all-absorbing cotton-wool touched each palm in turn, and Edward felt that the last sully of his embrace, the last lingering kiss he had imprinted on those hands had been washed into the abyss of nothingness."

Such is the amazing power of the redeeming blood of Christ which comes into our lives so mercifully, so humanly. The Sacraments work their healing upon us in ways that are infinitely beyond our comprehension, but always they give us a clear reassurance of what they are accomplishing. Modern science has discovered so-called miracle drugs which seem to conquer almost every kind of physical ill. Their power is great, yet it is insignificant when compared with the power of the Sacraments, which search out and remedy every last spiritual deformity or infirmity. We must understand clearly and always just what the Sacraments can accomplish; but more important still is the determination that what they can do, they will someday do for us, that they will prepare us for everlasting nearness to God.

# The Unending Sacrifice

DURING THE CENTURIES THAT PRECEDED THE coming of Christ, the religions of the world presented a very confused appearance. There was the one true God, there was a people dedicated to Him, there were sacrifices prescribed by Him. But all this that was true and good was like a small island in the midst of a turbulent ocean. All about, there were false gods and false religions; there were countless forms of sacrifice, ranging from human sacrifice to the pouring out of water upon the ground; there were innumerable opinions as to what God commanded and what He forbade. If there had been students of comparative religion in those days, they might very well have been quite confused and bewildered. Plutarch described conditions quite correctly when he wrote: "You may find cities without walls, without literature, and without arts and sciences of civilized life, but you will never find a city without priests and altars, on which sacrifices are offered to the gods."

Christ came into the world, and all this confusion melted

away. Christ offered to God the one, all-perfect Sacrifice, the
Sacrifice of the Cross. He prescribed that this Sacrifice should
be renewed for all time and in all places, right down to the
end of the world. Christ did not assemble armies. He did not
command His followers to go out and conquer and destroy
the false gods and false religions. Rather, He commissioned
them to teach and to live His religion, knowing that this
would be the surest deathblow to error and evil. Centuries
before, this had been predicted by the Prophet Malachias:
"From the rising of the sun even to the going down, my name
is great among the Gentiles, and in every place there is sacrifice, and there is offered in my name a clean oblation" (Mal.
1:10–11). The Sacrifice of the Mass is that oblation.

All that the Mass has in the way of importance and value
and dignity comes to it from the Sacrifice which Christ
offered upon the cross. In fact, if God had so desired, that one
all-perfect Sacrifice, offered on the first Good Friday, could
have been all that would be offered to God. God could have
disposed things in this manner, but He decided otherwise. He
knew how very easy it is for us to forget even the things
which have been most strongly impressed upon us. He knew
how vague and unreal are the events of past centuries, if we
know them only by word of mouth. He wanted His Sacrifice
to be very real in our lives, and so He commanded that it
would be renewed and perpetuated at all times and among
every people. It was to be not for the few but for everyone.
Even when it would be ignored or unknown, it would still
be available when men would realize their need of it. People
could go on their way concerned only with their money,
their business, or their pleasure, but always ready for them
to turn to it would be the Sacrifice of the Mass.

Bruce Marshall, in *Father Malachy's Miracle*, pictures the

offering of Mass in a church located in a busy city in Scotland. He describes how the priest "crossed himself as though he were tracing upon his soul the agony of Our Saviour's passion and death and moved through the whole glorious mystery with the reverence and the dignity of a boy who had been ordained the day before and with the lingering affection of a holy old man who must die that night." He describes the few who were present at that weekday Mass, and those who passed by outside. "Outside the trams, red, lusty, and agnostic, clanged by. Outside the great kaleidoscope kept turning and men and women, with bowler hats and powder puffs and Pekinese dogs to hide their immortal souls, went solemnly about their important unimportances. Outside Edinburgh continued to be bleak, (Protestant) and to lead countries which had never heard of it in science, philosophy, medicine, and respectability. But inside the Church of Saint Margaret of Scotland, perched like a supernatural toad between a music hall and a doubtful lodging house, Father Malachy stood at the altar of God and traced once more the epic of Our Lord's Crucifixion. To the left he moved, to the centre and to the right, and always slowly and gently as though his feet would do penance for the helter-skelter of modern men. And back to the centre again and on into the deep sea of the Mass where, with Peter and Paul, Simon and Thaddeus, Cosmas and Damian like rocks about him, he bent and brought God to bread amid an unheard fluttering of unseen wings."

Through many strange and devious paths, the Sacrifice of the Mass has come down to us through the intervening years. At the Last Supper, there were the twelve Apostles watching with breathless wonder as Christ took bread, blessed it, and broke it, saying: "This is my Body"; and as He took the chalice with the wine, blessed it, and gave it to them, saying:

"This is my Blood of the New Testament, which shall be shed for you and for many unto the remission of sins." There was a mixture of friends and foes, saints and sinners, when, on the following day, Christ offered up the Sacrifice of the Cross. There were those like His Blessed Mother who watched with deepest faith and reverence as they beheld that Sacrifice being offered by the Son of God; there were those who turned from their disbelief at the sight of this marvel and cried out: "Indeed this was the Son of God"; and there were those who came and watched, and walked indifferently away, totally unaffected by it all.

There on Calvary itself was set the pattern that mankind was to follow in its attitude toward the Mass. When the Mass was offered in the catacombs, and men and women risked torture and death for the privilege of being present at this Sacrifice, there were so many who walked back and forth in the streets overhead, not only indifferent but even eager to desecrate and destroy this great mystery. When the Church was able to come into the open, it was still the same — those who came with understanding and faith and reverence; and those who would neither see nor believe. Even today, whether there are the few or whether there are the many thousands who kneel to offer once again the Sacrifice of the Mass, the coldness and the indifference and the hatred is always just outside in the shadow. From Calvary right unto the end of time, the Mass will always be offered up, a Sacrifice unto God. We, and all who will see what we see, will have a part in that Sacrifice; those who remain outside will deny what they cannot see, and hate what they will never understand. It is an unending mystery, the mystery of God's love and patience, the mystery of man's ability to destroy what would have saved him.

# Watching One Hour

ONE OF THE MOST AMAZING THINGS ABOUT the life that Christ lived in this world is the fact that He was so very human. If we realize that He is God, with all the infinite powers of God, without being restricted by any of our human limitations, it becomes almost incredible that He could have entered so intimately into human life. St. Paul felt that he could describe the life of our Lord by saying: "He became like unto us in all things, sin alone excepted." However, there was a greater difference between the life of Christ and our life than would at first meet the eye. What we are and what we do can be of lasting importance, but never in the same way or to the same extent as the life and actions of Christ.

This is particularly true of the sufferings which we endure in the course of our lifetime. Properly accepted, they can be of unending value and worth. Christ's sufferings, however, were not merely of infinite worth, but they had a certain immortal quality about them which has made them alive and vital in every period of human history, and has made them a part of all Christian sufferings.

In the very earliest days of the Church, Saul, the fiery zealot who felt that he was doing a service to God by his persecution of the Christians, was dramatically shown his mistake. It was made clear to him that he was not merely persecuting his fellow men. He was persecuting Christ. Just as Saul felt that he would soon be able to exterminate the whole band of Christians, he was suddenly stricken on the way to Damascus. He was blinded. He fell from his horse. And he heard the voice of Christ reproaching him: "Saul, Saul, why persecutest thou me?" . . . "I am Christ whom thou persecutest." The earthly life of Christ was over at that time. Our Saviour had risen from the dead and ascended into heaven; and yet, somehow, He was still suffering, still undergoing persecution.

It was quite similar with the Apostle Peter. A story which goes back to the early centuries relates that St. Peter came to Rome to combat the errors of Simon the magician. Dissension was stirred up, and Peter's life was in danger. The Apostle felt it necessary to leave the city, but as he was leaving the city, Christ appeared to him. Peter, with his lifelong impetuosity, asked Christ: "Lord, where are you going?" The Lord answered: "I am going to Rome to be crucified again." Peter understood at once. He must not fear suffering or flee from it, and even if he must suffer and die, he will not be alone. Christ will be with him.

This has always been the true idea of Christian suffering. That is why the followers of Christ have never felt the full devastating force of human misery and misfortune. They have meditated upon, they have shared in the sufferings of Christ, and Christ, in return, has entered into and alleviated their sufferings.

Helen White, in one of her novels, has well portrayed this mystery. The story, *A Watch In The Night*, presents the life of the Franciscan monk, Jacopone da Todi. This man passes through a series of sufferings that try his faith and his patience, and when he has emerged into the peace that offers itself as the reward of suffering, he is able to advise and help others. He comes to a plague-stricken village, and speaks to the wretched sufferers.

"I fancy that there is nobody here who has not often thought when he heard that Gospel read in the church each year that if he had the privilege of watching with Our Lord that night, he would not have slept like St. John and St. Peter. You have often said to yourself, 'If I had been there, I would have kept awake with Our Blessed Lord, I would have wept with Him, I would have comforted His pain and His fear.' You have all said this to yourself, thinking always that this happened a long time ago, and that it is too bad that you did not live then. But tonight it is given to you to share this watch with your Lord, and He is sharing it with you. . . . Oh my brethren, there is nothing which He has asked you to bear this night which He has not Himself known in the flesh even as you know it now. There is nothing of this pain this night which He has not borne before, which He does not bear now. For He has borne pain and fever and thirst and grief in all His members, and He has borne it for you. . . . O my brethren, however long this night for you it will have an ending. And for you, He will say what He said to the thief on the cross, 'This night thou shalt walk with Me in Paradise.' In Paradise, my brethren, where the stones will no longer be hard under your aching head, where the naked sky will be warm and sweet in the sun of God's presence, and you will drink of waters that will never cease to flow sweet and cool, and you will walk in sunny fields with bodies light as air, and your hearts will sing with the joy of those who are at home forever in their Father's house.

"But for Him, my brethren, there is no death coming with great releasing wings to bear Him unto rest. So long as one human soul lives and sins upon this earth, so long as one body is racked with pain, and one soul is tortured with guilt and fear, He is afever and athirst and afraid. It is one hour only that He asks you to watch with Him. And as He comes here to you tonight, He asks you, 'Can you not watch with Me one hour?' O my brethren, answer, 'Yes,' to Him, for this night you are watching with your Lord, and tomorrow night you will walk with Him in Paradise."

This is not the ordinary or even the natural attitude toward suffering. It is not a condition of things that had to be, or even a condition of things that we would have expected. It is something which God has provided for us by His own free choice and because of His concern for us. When people criticize God for allowing suffering to remain in this world, they are criticizing a type of suffering which God neither wishes nor intends. He does not wish people to be distressed and overburdened and made desperate by the heavy weight of pain. He knows, as all the saints have known, that we never need to bear suffering in this way. If it is endured with Christ and for Christ and out of love for Christ it will never drag us down beyond our strength or our endurance. The Apostle summed it up perfectly: "I can bear all things in him who strengtheneth me."

History reminds us of many men who have endured with

courage and with patience very heavy burdens of suffering. It is encouraging for us to know the deep reserves of human strength and endurance. But, the help that this can give to us is seldom of much avail in the crises of our own life. There, if our own strength should falter, the example of others however heroic is not likely to be of much avail. It is only the sufferings of Christ that can bring us the strength, the faith, the hope, and the love of God which lead to victory.

# The Other Sheep

IN OUR DEALINGS WITH OUR FELLOW MEN, IT is often hard to draw the line between sincere Christian interest in others and curiosity about their personal affairs, between a zealous desire to help them and interference in what does not concern us. The principles of Christian charity are very simple and clear, but their application is not always so easy. Even the Apostles at times experienced this difficulty. This is well brought out in the incident related in St. John's Gospel concerning God's plans for the Apostles Peter and John. After our Lord's resurrection from the dead, He won from Peter a threefold protestation of love and loyalty and set him as head of the newly established Church. Then, He foretold what Peter would have to endure. " 'When thou wast young thou didst gird thyself and walk where thou wouldst. But when thou art old thou wilt stretch forth thy hands, and another will gird thee, and lead thee where thou wouldst not.' Now this he said to signify by what manner of death he should glorify God. And having spoken thus, he said to him, 'Follow me.' Turning round, Peter saw following them the disciple whom Jesus loved . . . Peter therefore, seeing him, said to Jesus, 'Lord, and what of this man?' Jesus said to him, 'If I wish him to remain until I come, what is it to thee? Do thou follow me'" (Jn. 21:18–22). It was not a particularly sharp or serious rebuke that our Lord thus gave to the Apostle Peter. He was simply reminding him that God does not intend to reveal to us all of His purposes and intentions as regards our fellow men.

Down through the Christian centuries, many men have been preoccupied with a similar though broader problem. What of the people who never come to a knowledge of Christ? What of people who are of good heart but never have the opportunity to know the truths which our Lord has revealed? How will the Passion of Christ profit people who have never even heard of it? How will God act toward people in this predicament? Will they be saved, and if so, how? It is a vast problem. Christ, during His years in this world, preached to many people that numbered only in the thousands. There were millions who never heard Him or even heard about Him. His Apostles were sent out to preach the Gospel to the whole world, but at their death the world was still far from being Christian. Now, after 1900 years of Christianity, statistics show that out of the two billion, four hundred million people in this world, less than one fifth are Catholics and less than one third are Christians of any kind. It is a problem, and whether or not it is our problem, people have concerned themselves about the answer.

In *The Other Wise Man*, Henry Van Dyke proposes a partial solution. He builds his story about the Wise Men who came from the East to worship the newborn Christ. The fourth Wise Man or the "other" Wise Man is named Artaban. He has a rendezvous with the three Wise Men. He has prepared to set out and has disposed of his house and posses- sions, using the money to purchase three precious stones which he intends to present to the King he is to worship. As soon as he can, he speeds on his way to join the other Wise Men. He is almost at his destination when he meets a stranger lying sick on the highway. He stops to alleviate his wants and in doing so, he is so long delayed that the caravan of the Wise Men leaves without him and sets out across the wastes of the desert. Artaban cannot follow on horseback. He must sell one of his precious stones to purchase a caravan of his own for the long dangerous journey to Judea. When he arrives at Bethlehem, the other Wise Men have already been there and gone. Herod's soldiers arrive while he is there. Artaban uses another of his precious stones to bribe a soldier to spare the life of one of the boy children of Bethlehem. Then, he sets out for Egypt, still following the Infant Christ. The journey continues on and on, discouraging but never abandoned.

After thirty years, Artaban is finally once more in the foot- steps of Christ. He arrives in Jerusalem and finds the city in a tumult. He is given the reason. "We are going to the place called Golgotha, outside the city walls, where there is to be an execution. Have you not heard what has happened? Two famous robbers are to be crucified, and with them another, called Jesus of Nazareth, a man who has done many wonder- ful works among the people, so that they love Him greatly. But the priests and elders have said that He must die, because He gave Himself out to be the Son of God. And Pilate has sent Him to the cross because He said that He was the 'King of the Jews'."

"Artaban's heart beat unsteadily with that troubled, doubtful apprehension which is the excitement of old age. But he said within himself: 'The ways of God are stranger than the thoughts of men, and it may be that I shall find the King, at last, in the hands of His enemies, and shall come in time to offer my pearl for His ransom before He dies.'" He sets out with some of his old hope swelling strong within him. But once again, there is the interruption and apparent frustration. A young girl about to be sold into slavery to satisfy the debts of her father beseeches his help. The last of Artaban's precious stones is spent in her ransom. And then, it is the moment of Christ's death. A violent earthquake rocks the whole city. A sharp stone falls from a roof upon Artaban. He falls, bleeding and dying, to the ground. The girl whom he has rescued is privileged to hear the welcome which Christ extends to this departed soul as he goes into eternity. Artaban is overwhelmed by the loving gratitude with which his Master receives him. "When saw I Thee hungered and fed Thee? or thirsty, and gave Thee drink? When saw I Thee a stranger, and took Thee in? Or naked, and clothed Thee? When saw I Thee sick or in prison and came unto Thee? Three-and-thirty years have I looked for Thee; but I have never seen Thy face, nor ministered to Thee, my King." And then comes that reply, so richly laden with God's mercy, "Verily I say unto thee, inasmuch as thou hast done it unto one of the least of these My brethren, thou hast done it unto Me."

It is rash and it is mistaken to put limits to God's mercy. We know the ordinary means of grace which God has established, the Church, prayer, the Sacraments, a knowledge of the sufferings and death of Christ. We know how great a privilege it is to have these means at our disposal. We know the serious obligation of understanding Christ's teachings, applying them to our life, using all the helps which He has made available to us. For us, it is the only way of ordering our lives. But who can say what God may do for those who are unable to know what we know, those who would always like to come to Christ, but through no fault of their own always seem to miss Him. They may never kneel before His crib at Christmas, they may never stand beneath His cross on Good Friday, they may never behold His empty tomb on Easter morning, but if they have sincerely sought Him all this time, may they not still find Him at life's closing? We do not know. God has not told us. Perhaps He does tell us: "What is it to thee? Do *thou* follow Me!"